APR   2007

The Complete Book of
Glass Beadmaking

Kimberley Adams

LARK BOOKS

A Division of Sterling Publishing Co., Inc.
New York

Editor: **Katherine Duncan Aimone**
Art Director: **Kathleen Holmes**
Cover Designer: **Barbara Zaretsky**
Assistant Editor: **Rebecca Guthrie**
Associate Art Director: **Shannon Yokeley**
Photographer: **Keith Wright**
Editorial Assistance: **Delores Gosnell**
Editorial Intern: **Metta L. Pry**

I would like to dedicate this book to my children, Ian and Jordan, who keep me motivated and challenged every day. I couldn't do what I do without their continuous amazement over the art form that has become my passion.

Library of Congress Cataloging-in-Publication Data

Adams, Kimberley (Kimberley Ann), 1960-
        The complete book of glass beadmaking / Kimberley Adams.
            p. cm.
        Includes index.
        ISBN 1-57990-572-2 (hardcover)
        1. Glass craft.   2. Glass blowing and working.   3. Glass beads.   I. Title.
TT298.A33 2005
748.8'5—dc22

                            2005004908

10 9 8 7 6 5 4

Published by Lark Books, A Division of Sterling Publishing Co., Inc.
387 Park Avenue South, New York, N.Y. 10016

© 2005, Lark Books

Text © 2005, Kimberley Adams
Photography © 2005, Lark Books
Illustrations © 2005, Lark Books

Distributed in Canada by Sterling Publishing, c/o Canadian Manda Group, 165 Dufferin Street Toronto,
Ontario, Canada M6K 3H6

Distributed in the United Kingdom by GMC Distribution Services,
Castle Place, 166 High Street, Lewes, East Sussex, England BN7 1XU

Distributed in Australia by Capricorn Link (Australia) Pty Ltd., P.O. Box 704, Windsor, NSW 2756 Australia

If you have questions or comments about this book, please contact:
Lark Books
67 Broadway
Asheville, NC 28801
(828) 253-0467

Manufactured in China

ISBN 13: 978-1-57990-572-9
ISBN 10: 1-57990-572-2

For information about custom editions, special sales, premium and corporate purchases, please contact
Sterling Special Sales Department at 800-805-5489 or specialsales@sterlingpub.com.

All beads shown on the front cover are by Kimberley Adams, with the exception of the vessel bead design by Kate Fowle Meleney and the floral bead designs by Deanna Griffin Dove. The kaleidoscope bead shown was made by Kimberley Adams, but it is a design developed by Deanna Griffin Dove.

All other beads (back cover, spine, flaps, and contents page) are by Kimberley Adams.

Contents

Introduction

Glass is an amazing and mysterious material that has fascinated me all of my life. When I was a child, I collected colorful glass bottles and lovingly placed them on my windowsill. Sitting in church, I stared with awe at the beautiful patterns and designs of stained glass windows. Later, I was intrigued with blown glass vases and figures that my parents had brought to me as a gift from a trip through West Virginia, and I loved watching lampworkers create small figurines in the local mall.

As a young adult, I met artists who had their own glass studio. It was there that I tried my hand at blowing glass, and I still have some of my first awkward attempts at making small vessels.

Later, I had an opportunity to work with glass at the torch, and I immediately fell in love with it! From the moment I began, I was hooked. And the fact that everything was small and portable was very attractive—there were no big furnaces and ovens to deal with. This scaled-down version of working with hot glass fit perfectly into my busy lifestyle.

Today I teach lots of students and am still a perpetual student. I love teaching them to move from the first step of lighting a torch (which is a bit scary at first) to actually forming and decorating a bead. Each time I introduce a new person to beadmaking, it takes me back to my very first experiences and the moment when I said—WOW! Watching students at the torch, mesmerized by the exciting properties of glass, continues to inspire me.

I know that making your first beads will also excite and intrigue you. This very user-friendly book guides you through the basic steps of making a bead all the way through some of the most advanced techniques in use today. It tells you what I've learned through years of studying with other teachers, as well as the personal discoveries I've made. Very detailed how-to steps and close-up photos give you the information that you need to be successful in every realm of beadmaking.

In addition to this, you'll learn from two well-known artists and teachers—Kate Fowle Meleney and Deanna Griffin Dove. Kate's section introduces you to making beautiful sculptural beads, and Deanna gives you a look at the unlimited possibilities of "painting" on beads with glass to create floral beads.

You'll notice that the book begins by introducing you to the tools, equipment, and supplies you'll need as well as how to set up your own studio. The techniques are arranged from the simplest to most complex—from making the first bead, to decorating it with a myriad of surface treatments, to making complex canes. The book is also punctuated with inspiring images of beads by accomplished bead-makers, giving you a springboard for future ideas.

Beadmaking is all about experimentation, and after you've learned quite a bit and feel comfortable working with glass, you'll no doubt find yourself thinking, "…hey, but what if I tried this or that together?" Not everything will work, but try things out anyway. Combining different techniques is part of the fun of beadmaking.

After you've become an accomplished beadmaker, it's my hope that you'll keep this book on your studio shelf as a reference tool and a source of inspiration. I feel fortunate and honored to serve as your guide as you embark on your journey into this stimulating and ever-evolving world.

Kimberley Adams

Previous page, top: Kimberley Adams
Ocean Necklace, 2005
45.7 cm long
Lampworked; soda-lime glass; various techniques

Previous page, center: Kate Fowle Meleney
Aegean Urn, 2005
7.5 x 1.5 cm
Lampworked; gold foil, enamel, murrini and etched

Previous page, bottom: Kimberley Adams
Untitled, 2004
Lampworked; pink bead fumed with gold on sterling silver wire finding, twisted dot

Top: Kimberley Adams
Autumn, 2004
116.8 cm long
Various techniques and handmade findings

Left: Deanna Griffin Dove
Vines, 2005
Various dimensions
Lampworked; soda-lime glass, raised stringer and raked dots

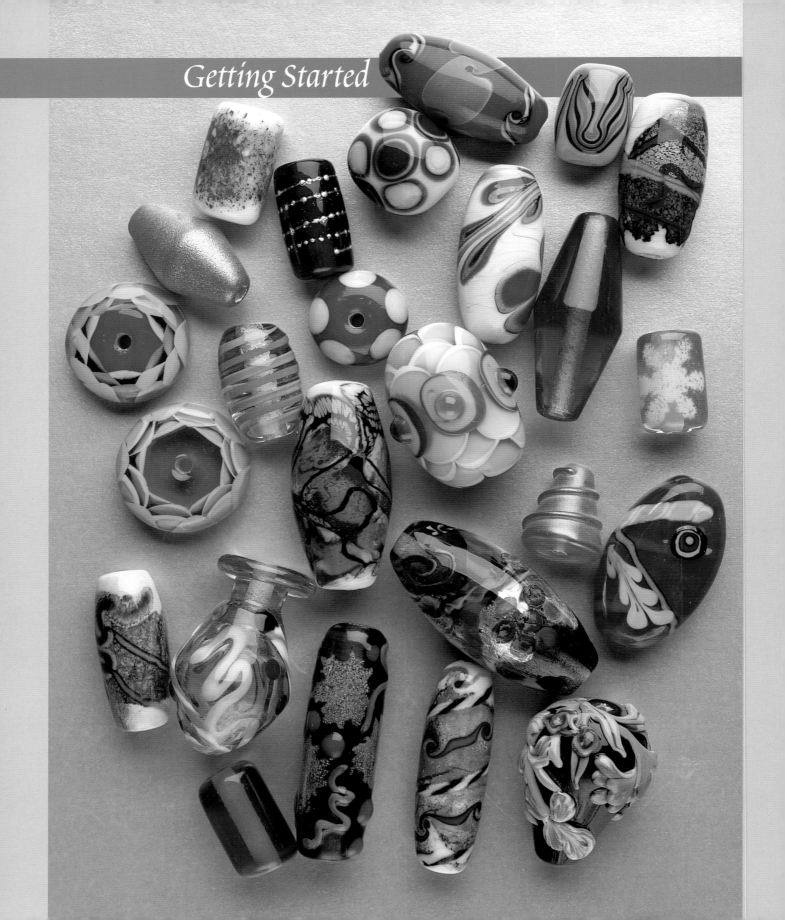

This chapter introduces you to all of the tools, supplies, and materials used throughout this book. Even though you can set up your studio in the beginning with nothing more than a torch and a few basic tools, you'll naturally add more to your stock as you learn.

Because glass beadmaking is more popular than ever, there are now many suppliers from which to choose. You can buy things you need at bead shops as well as stained glass suppliers. If you live in an area where there isn't a shop that you can visit, the Internet is a great resource. But don't get carried away! Begin with the things that you need and selectively choose from the rest. Remember, your focus in the beginning is on learning to work with the glass, and then you can reward yourself as you move on to more complex techniques.

As you read this chapter, which can serve as a reference for you as you work and learn, your choices for setting up your studio will become clearer. The pluses and minuses of various items described will assist you in making decisions. And, of course, the central part of your operation will be the torch that you choose, although you don't have to buy the most expensive one in the beginning.

If you are already making beads, you may not need to read this chapter, but there might be some nuggets of information in it that are helpful. For instance, the issue of safety in the studio is covered extensively. After you're set up, you won't cloud your wonderful experiences in the studio with a burn or a respiratory problem. And, we've added a special section on ergonomics in the studio.

Setting up a studio may seem arduous at first, but once you have a basic setup, you'll have a playground for creativity at your disposal. Making beads is so exciting, challenging, and energizing that, hopefully, you'll find yourself spending a lot of time there! Enjoy the process.

Equipment

In the following section, you'll learn about the fundamental equipment used in a beadmaking studio. A lot of this technical information can be daunting at first, but we have made it palatable and easy to understand. Always ask for help from an expert when you need it.

Torches

Several torches are appropriate for making beads with soft glass. These torches vary in design as well as price. Some of the more expensive torches are designed to produce more heat for working with *borosilicate (hard) glass*, but for the purpose of working with soft glass, the torches described in this section are more than adequate.

Before you invest in this piece of equipment, think about how and where you'll be using it. Does your torch need to be easy to move due to space considerations? And, if you're a beginner, you might want to invest in a less expensive torch.

Single-Fuel Torch

The simplest setup is the single-fuel torch, and this is often the choice of beginning beadmakers. This type of torch is designed to work with a propylene brazing fuel (a multi-purpose industrial fuel gas, MAPP) that comes in a disposable canister. This torch doesn't require an oxygen tank like other torches

used for beadmaking. The torch burns clean and is designed specifically to work with soft glass. It works in part by drawing in air through holes on the side of it. This uptake adds enough oxygen to the flame to heat the glass and work with it in a molten state without burning it. The flame is cooler than that of a more complex dual-fuel torch (described on page 9), which can be advantageous if you're learning to work with molten glass. The glass stays slightly stiffer in the flame, allowing you to work at a slower pace.

One small disadvantage of this simple torch is that the flame can be trickier to adjust than that of a more expensive one. Also, when you work with it, you'll notice that it makes a rushing sound after it is lit, created by fuel being dispensed through the head.

Brazing fuel for this torch is available from most home improvement supply or hardware stores in one-pound (.454 kg) non-refillable tanks that

can be clamped directly to your tabletop. You can also use larger, refillable tanks for brazing fuel that are available through welding suppliers. Using refillable tanks is a more economical and ecologically responsible approach, since you won't be throwing out empty tanks.

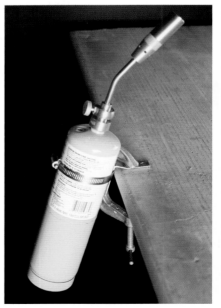

A single-fuel torch is an economical choice for beginning beadmakers.

If you use the disposable tank, you'll screw the torch directly into the top of it. The tank can be secured to the edge of your worktable using a large hose clamp along with an L-bracket and C-clamp. All of these items can be purchased from a home improvement supply store. Point the head of the torch away from you, and bend the bracket so that the torch (and therefore the flame) is angled forward.

You can also purchase a stand that attaches to your worktable that makes it easier to remove and replace tanks. These are available through beadmaking suppliers.

If you're using a refillable tank, ask your supplier to provide you with an appropriate hose and fitting or adapter. Then use a smaller hose clamp to hold the fitting, which is then attached to the tabletop with an L-bracket and C-clamp. The tank should be chained to a leg of your worktable so that it doesn't tip over, preventing possible damage to the valve on top of it. The hose should only be long enough to reach from the tabletop to the top of the tank so that you can reach it in case of an unexpected leak or emergency and close it off quickly.

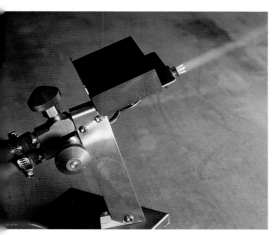

A duel-fuel torch uses oxygen and propane. It creates more heat than a single-fuel torch.

Dual-Fuel Torch

A torch with gas fuel (usually propane) and oxygen produces a much hotter flame than a single-fuel torch. The oxygen works as an accelerator by increasing the flame's temperature. The flame is also easier to adjust for detail work and creating a special atmosphere in the flame. The mix of oxygen to propane can be changed in order to coax special reactions in the glass.

These torches come in two types: *surface mix* and *internal mix or premix*. For working with soft glass, you'll use a surface-mix torch—named such because the fuels meet and combust at the end of the torch head. These torches require lower gas pressure than internal-mix torches, which are designed to create hotter, more intense flames that work well for making larger work and/or working with borosilicate (hard) glass. Surface-mix torches also produce enough heat to work with borosilicate, but they're not ideal.

Surface-mix torches vary greatly in price. The simplest kind has a single head with a torch head about $3/8$ inch (9.5 mm) wide. Other surface-mix torches have a second larger head or a ring of portals that make them capable of quickly melting greater amounts of glass or keeping larger beads hot. These torches allow you to switch back and forth between the smaller and larger flame as needed. The larger head produces enough heat to work easily with borosilicate glass. These torches are fixed on a base that is bolted or clamped to the tabletop. The positioning or angle of the torch is adjustable.

Hoses

The dual-fuel torch requires hoses that supply the oxygen and propane. These hoses can be purchased as an attached set or as two separate hoses. Green is always used for the oxygen, and red for the propane. Fittings should be attached to one end of each of the hoses. A fitting with a left-hand thread is always used for the propane (red) hose, and a fitting with a right-hand thread is used for the oxygen (green). This distinction protects you from making incorrect connections from the torch to the tank.

If you purchase hoses from a bead-making supplier, the fittings will already be attached to one end of the hoses. If you're working with a welding supplier, ask for assistance in adding the fittings.

The other end of the hose has no fitting and is attached to the torch. Slip a small hose clamp over this end of the hose before slipping it onto the torch, which has a barbed fitting. After the hose has been pushed all the way over this fitting, slide the hose clamp over that area and tighten it down.

If you have any trouble attaching the hoses to your torch, ask a welding supplier (who will be supplying your oxygen) for assistance in making secure connections.

Check Valve/
Flashback Arrestor

To the fitted end of the hoses, you'll add a set of safety devices—either a *check valve* or a *flashback arrestor*. When working with a surface-mix torch, a lower-priced check valve is sufficient since this torch is much less likely to flashback than an internal-mix torch.

A *flashback* occurs when the flame burns back into the torch, hoses, and possibly the tanks. Obviously, this can be an explosive situation. Most often it happens when the tip of the torch becomes blocked, preventing the flow of gases.

A check valve keeps gas flowing in one direction—away from the tank. A flashback arrestor is basically a check valve with an additional safety component for extinguishing a possible flame. These devices are attached between the regulator and hose, and like the hoses, those made for use with oxygen have a right-hand thread, and those made for use with propane have a left-hand thread.

A check valve fitted to the end of a hose

Regulators

Check valves or flashback arrestors are in turn attached to a set of regulators. A dual-gauged regulator is connected to the oxygen tank, and a single-gauged one is used for the propane. Both are available through your welding or beadmaking supplier.

The oxygen regulator is made to withstand the higher pressure of oxygen. This regulator has two gauges—one describes the pressure in the tank, the other indicates the oxygen's rate of flow to the torch. Be sure to purchase one that's calibrated to clearly read low pressure, since you'll be using only eight to 12 psi (pounds per square inch).

Before attaching the regulator to the oxygen tank, be sure that the valve (which has a right-hand thread) is clean and free of dirt or debris. Secure the tank where you want it to be, and position the valve opening pointing away from you. To open the tank, turn the top valve and release a quick burst of oxygen. Then quickly close off the valve again.

Attach the regulator to the top of the tank by screwing it onto the threaded valve. Tighten the fitting by hand, and use a crescent wrench to snug it down on the tank. Be careful not to screw it on so tightly that you strip the brass threads on the fitting, which can lead to leaks. A description of testing for leaks and how to fix them will be discussed later (see page 12).

When purchasing a propane regulator, be sure to purchase one that's also calibrated to clearly read low pressure, as is your oxygen regulator. Generally, you'll be using between four and eight psi. A propane regulator is also designed with the reverse, or left-hand, threading, so that only a propane tank can be used with it. (Again, this left-hand thread is designed into all the propane fittings—from the tank to regulator to check valve and to fittings on the hose.)

Before attaching the propane regulator to the tank, quickly open the valve to allow gas to blow out any debris before closing it back down again. Do this in a well-ventilated area, away from an open flame. Then screw the regulator onto the fitting on top of the propane tank. Tighten it by hand as much as possible, followed by a crescent wrench to make it snug. Be careful not to strip the threads of the brass fittings, since this can cause leaks.

A dual-gauged regulator, attached to an oxygen tank, controls the flow of oxygen to the torch.

Oxygen and Propane Tanks

You'll be working with two tanks, so you'll need to place them where they're safe and won't tip over or get damaged. Chain the oxygen tank to a wall or stationary object. Neither tank should be close to any open flame. Ideally, place the propane tank outside and run the hose inside your studio to the torch.

You can rent or purchase an oxygen tank from an oxygen supplier. The tank size you choose depends on how often you plan to work on the torch and what your supplier can deliver to your studio. Since transporting them yourself is dangerous and cumbersome, it's best to get them delivered. Get tanks that are of a size that you're able to move (roll) on your own. It's a good idea to have two or three tanks delivered at a time so you'll always have oxygen available. Work with your supplier to come up with a delivery schedule that fits your budget and the amount of oxygen you use.

Any extra tanks should be stored upright with the caps screwed on, chained to a stationary object or wall, and protected from the weather. Always keep the caps on them until you're ready to connect them to the regulator. Oxygen alone isn't flammable, but it is an accelerant, and therefore causes things to burn. Never store anything oily near the tanks, and never use oil on the tanks, since this combination can be potentially dangerous.

Although propane is available in tanks of various sizes, small ones, such as one sized for an outdoor grill or smaller, are the right size for beadmaking. You can buy them at your local hardware store.

You won't use propane up as quickly as oxygen. The regulator for propane may only have one gauge for adjusting the gas pressure to the torch. If this is the case, the only way to tell how much propane is left in the tank is to weigh it. It's advisable to keep a backup tank handy.

Since propane is highly flammable, you should store it outside. (If a leak should develop on your tank, it is unsafe for your studio.) Because propane tanks are smaller, with a lower center of gravity than oxygen tanks, they're less likely to tip over. Nevertheless, it's still a good idea to secure them with a chain or chord to a wall.

Anytime you plan to be away from your torch for some time, you'll need to bleed the line from the propane tank to your torch. To do this, turn off the oxygen valve at the tank first, and then turn off the propane valve at the tank. Light the torch (propane only) so that it continues to burn until all the propane is gone from the line. When the flame has burned out, turn off the propane valve at your torch. Then bleed the oxygen line by opening the valve at the torch. As the oxygen leaves the line, it will help disseminate any residual propane.

Oxygen tanks should be chained to a wall for safety.

Store propane tanks outside your studio.

Adjusting the Flow

Once the entire system is connected, it's time to establish the flow of oxygen and propane. Be sure that all your connections are tight—from the tank, to the regulator, to the check valve or flashback arrestor, to the hose, and to the torch. On each regulator, make sure that the adjustment handle is opened out all the way—turned counterclockwise, so that the pressure of the gases won't hit the spring valve inside the regulator. (This is more important on the oxygen regulator, since oxygen is stored under high pressure.)

On the propane tank, open the valve on the top about three quarters of a turn. (Opening the tank slightly allows you to close the tank quickly in case of a leak or fire.) Then screw down the adjustment handle until the flow of gas begins. Continue to turn this handle until the psi reads about four.

When opening the valve on the oxygen tank, you should avoid standing in front of it. Open the valve at the top of the tank as slowly as possible, so that the inner workings of the regulator aren't hit with a sudden pressure increase. Such increases can deteriorate regulator valves over time and cause them to fail. Open the tank valve all the way to properly seat it and avoid leaks. The gauge showing the tank's pressure (usually on the right) should give a reading when the tank is first opened. A full tank should register around 2000 psi. This gauge helps you keep track of the amount of oxygen in the tank.

Next, screw down the adjustment handle until the second gauge on the left begins to read the flow of oxygen. This gauge shows you the rate at which the oxygen is dispensed from the tank. Continue to turn the adjustment handle until the gauge reads about 10 psi. If it is adjusted too high, open the valve on the torch, allow oxygen to flow from it, and lower the psi to the desired flow.

Checking for Leaks

Once the flow of oxygen and propane is established, it's extremely important to check for possible leaks between all connections in the system. To do this, fill a spray bottle with liquid leak detection solution. This solution can be purchased from a welding, beadmaking, or flameworking supplier, or you can mix a weak solution of water and dish soap. The soap should not contain petroleum, since such products can spontaneously combust if they come in contact with oxygen.

Check every connection from the tank (propylene brazing fuel, oxygen, or propane)—from regulator to hose to torch—anywhere a metal fitting is used. Spray each connection with enough solution to soak it. If

Leak detection fluid sprayed onto connectors will bubble up, indicating a gas leak. This is a safety measure that must be taken when you set up your system as well as periodically while you're working.

there is a leak, bubbles will form around the connection. Try tightening the connection again and then retest it.

If you still have a leak, you can use a tape specifically designed to stop leaks around the threads of connections (available from a welding supplier). Wrap it around the threaded part of the male fitting in the direction of the threads before wrapping the tape around and onto itself. Attach the connection again, and then check for leaks once more.

If a leak persists, that connection point might need to be replaced by your welding supplier.

Alternatives for Fueling Your Studio

The following section explains how you can use an oxygen generator instead of constantly restocking your studio with tanks. There are pros and cons to this kind of setup. And, if you have access to natural gas, it can serve as a substitute for propane.

Oxygen Concentrator or Generator

These machines, usually used in a medical setting, pull oxygen from existing air in a room. Beadmakers have adapted them for use as an alternative to oxygen tanks, eliminating a lot of inconvenience. An oxygen generator is a larger system with several interconnected components and produces more pressure than a single-component concentrator.

The initial cost of either machine is high, but pays for itself over time, since you don't have to buy tanks and refill them. The air supply to them must be clean and dry. Thus, machines used in humid areas might need filters and/or the addition of a dehumidifier to the room. The temperature of the workspace can also affect the machine's operation. For instance, if your workspace isn't heated continuously, you'll probably need to heat it before operating the machine. Maintenance is a must, and parts are quite expensive to replace.

The biggest difference, operationally, between a tank and a concentrator/generator is that the second choice provides a low psi of up to around 12. This is usually adequate for most soft-glass work

on surface-mix torches, and the lower pressure somewhat slows down the pace of beadmaking.

Used or reconditioned concentrators are available from medical equipment suppliers and are less expensive than new ones. Make certain that your supplier can also service the machine if needed. Use the same testing system for leaks as an oxygen tank.

Natural Gas

If you already have natural gas at your home or studio, it's possible to use this as a substitute for propane. If you choose this option, the flow of gas into your home or studio will probably need to be increased so that you have enough flow to service the torch. Then, you might need a flow reducer added to each gas appliance that you already have. Work with your gas supplier and a plumber to attach the fittings to your gas line and meet local codes to make sure that your system is safe and you have no leaks.

Cooling Equipment

Once you've made a glass bead at the torch, you must slowly cool the glass to avoid breakage from *thermal shock*. There are several ways to do this, as described below, that take the glass from molten, which is roughly 1700°F (927°C), to room temperature.

Larger beads, beads that have been encased, and beads with extended parts, such as handles, have to be put directly into a preheated kiln so that they cool properly (see page 15 for more information on kiln annealing). The following two methods allow you to cool most other beads to room temperature without having to heat up your kiln to anneal them right after they're made.

You can use one of two cooling methods for beads without heating up your kiln—fill pots with vermiculite or sandwich your beads in an insulated fiber blanket.

Fiber Blankets

Placing beads between two layers of a fiber blanket (with no asbestos content) is a simple way to slow down the cooling process. You can purchase one from a beadmaking supplier. It's a good idea to wrap the blanket in aluminum foil beforehand to prevent your hands from coming in contact with skin-irritating fibers. Since these blankets tend to deteriorate, they must be replaced fairly often.

NOTE

Cooling is slowed down only while the beads are covered. If you open up the "sandwich" to add another bead, you'll release stored heat, creating a quick variance and the possibility of thermal shock. To avoid this, quickly slip the bead inside the blanket.

Vermiculite

Vermiculite that has been preheated in a crock-pot or in a pot on a hotplate can also be used to effectively slow down the cooling of beads. (This mica-like material is commonly used to aerate soil, so you can buy it at a gardening store.) When the hot beads are pushed into this material, it serves as an insulator, and a pocket of heat is created. The vermiculite slowly disperses the heat.

You'll need a second container of vermiculite for the second stage of cooling the beads. Don't heat this container, but leave it at room temperature. Once you've cooled the beads in the preheated container for about 45 minutes, you'll move them to this one for further cooling until they reach room temperature. Be sure the vermiculite is deep enough that each bead is completely covered when plunged into the pot.

NOTE

Since there is some concern about the safety of breathing dust from vermiculite, be safe and pour it into your container outside, so that the dust blows away from you, or wear a dust mask. When you heat a crock-pot of vermiculite for the first time, place it underneath the ventilation system in your studio so that any dust and fumes are directly drawn out. You'll still have to stir it occasionally, so wear a dust mask when you do this. Replace the vermiculite when it begins to break down into smaller pieces.

Kiln for Cooling and Annealing Beads

Annealing is a process of slow and controlled cooling that prevents your glass from getting stressed and consequently cracked or broken due to uneven cooling. An *annealing kiln* is an insulated container (an oven of sorts) that allows you to control the temperature inside from room temperature to over 2000°F (1093°C). A kiln will probably be the most expensive piece of equipment that you buy for your studio. Using a small electric kiln is the most ideal way to cool your beads, because you'll be able to cool and anneal them in one cycle after you *flame-anneal* them at the torch (see page 41).

Some kilns made specifically for annealing beads have a small trap door that allows you to place the mandrel and bead into it without opening the main door and losing heat. We'll discuss kiln annealing in more depth later at the end of chapter 2 (see page 42).

An electric kiln is heated by a set of elements that carry an electrical charge. Because you'll be reaching into the heated kiln, look for one with elements covered in fiber or quartz tubing. Some contain elements pushed down into an L-shaped groove. Buy a kiln with elements installed so that you're not likely to touch them with a metal mandrel.

Protect your hands and arms when you reach into a hot kiln. Wear non-asbestos, high-temperature gloves. To protect your arms and upper body, wear heavy clothing of natural fiber. Synthetic fibers can melt and fuse to your skin, resulting in some nasty burns.

Inside the kiln, you'll need a way to support the mandrels rather than placing them on the bottom of the kiln. Use kiln furniture such as ceramic kiln posts and shelves from a ceramic supplier.

Gauging and Controlling the Kiln's Temperature

To anneal beads, your kiln must be equipped with a *pyrometer*, which is a high-temperature thermometer that reads the kiln's internal temperature. You'll also need some means of controlling the kiln's temperature. The simplest device is an *infinite control switch*—a switch that doesn't allow you to specify a particular temperature, only a general range. You'll need to work with your kiln for a while to figure out which settings on this high to low dial work for keeping the kiln at a certain temperature. Keep in mind that every time you

open the door of the kiln, you will lose some heat. Try to do this quickly so that you don't lose a lot of heat. And, of course, the more often you reach into the kiln, the more heat you'll lose. With only an infinite control switch, you will need to watch the temperature reading constantly and adjust it as needed.

A *set-point controller* is a device that will baby-sit the kiln for you, and keep the temperature within the range that you need. This device alleviates the necessity of watching the kiln. Some digital versions can be programmed for a careful cooling/annealing process based on the formula of glass used. While not inexpensive, they are well worth the money.

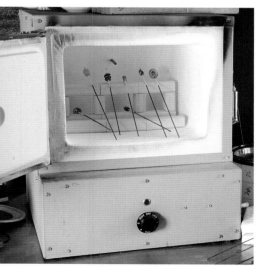

A small kiln is used for cooling and annealing beads, and ceramic kiln furniture is used to prop them up.

Tools

There are many tools available that are made specifically for beadmaking. Other tools are adapted from various disciplines such as woodworking and jewelry-making. You can also use common items that you have around your home. This section introduces you to the basic tools as well as some fancier ones that will be used throughout the book.

There are a few tools that you'll use almost every time you make simple beads, such as a *marver*, a graphite paddle, and some sort of tool for pinching the glass. As your skills develop, you'll need more tools. Buy what you need to get started. Then add to your collection, whether you buy things from a bead supplier or scavenge for them at a flea market.

The first section describes "shapers," or tools that you use to shape and mold the glass. The second section follows up with all of the support tools you'll need to assist you as you decorate beads.

Tools for shaping beads include (left to right): a graphite paddle, knives, needle-nose pliers, a tungsten probe, pointed tweezers, flat-ended (tabular) tweezers, a bead rake, and a selection of marvers

Shapers

All sorts of tools are used to shape beads—from a simple kitchen knife to those made specifically for this task. Over the years, beadmakers have adapted tools and refined them for shaping glass and creating patterns on its surface. Some of the tools described below are from the jeweler's bench, while others were adapted from glass blowing.

Marvers

Any surface that won't ignite or melt when a hot bead is rolled or pressed on it for shaping can be used as a marver. Most marvers are made from graphite or metal (such as stainless steel or aluminum). They can also be made of clay or stone and be smooth or patterned.

A graphite torch-top marver mounted on a stainless steel base close to the flame can be attached to the top of your torch. This warm surface cools the glass less than a regular room-temperature marver, allowing you more shaping time. This marver is also handy for preheating glass elements that will be added to your bead, such as *millefiori* (see page 105).

Graphite Paddles

This helpful tool, used for shaping molten glass, is made up of a flat piece of graphite attached to a wooden or rubber handle. It is similar to a marver, but you can use the paddle to shape glass more delicately and in more detail, since you can hold and manipulate this tool. Paddles come in many sizes and shapes. Some have flat or knife-like edges, while others have round or tapered ones to give your glass further definition.

Graphite works well with the glass for a couple of reasons: It doesn't absorb as much heat from the glass as metal does, and glass doesn't stick to graphite even when it gets hot. A paddle with a notch drilled into the side is helpful for holding a bead steady in the flame.

Occasionally, paddles are made from metal (usually brass). These are more resistant to chipping, particularly if they have a knife-edge. However, they are heavier and cool the glass much faster than graphite.

Pliers

Various kinds of pliers are used for pinching, shaping, and manipulating hot glass. You can buy a small pair of needle-nose pliers for some purposes, or buy pliers designed to suit specific purposes from a beadmaking supplier. Bent-nosed pliers, for instance, come in handy for pinching glass.

Some pliers have special attachments welded onto them for shaping molten glass into leaf-like shapes, creating grooves, or flattening.

More shaping tools (clockwise from the center) include: graphite shapers, pliers with special ends, a spackling tool, a parallel press, graphite rods, and patterned clay marvers

Parallel Press

This tool is composed of two parallel, flat metal plates attached to a U-shaped handle. Since these plates meet each other perfectly, you can use it to flatten or mash glass.

Bead Rake

A bead rake is a hooked metal tool used to create designs on the surface of a bead. Rakes are available from bead suppliers, or you can use a dental probe as a rake.

However, it is simple to make one from a thin *mandrel*. These are less expensive and easier to replace, plus you can use bent mandrels that are no longer useful for wrapping beads. File the end of the mandrel to a point, and bend about 1 inch (2.5 cm) of it at a 90° angle. The thinner the metal is on the rake, the more vulnerable it is to melting while you're using it, especially if you hold the rake in the flame.

Tweezers

Stainless-steel tweezers made for working with glass come in various lengths. You should have at least one pair that is 4 inches (10.2 cm) or longer. Tweezers are used to pinch, pull, and move glass around. You'll use them often to pull off and discard glass bits. A tabular design with a wider, flat area works well for picking up metal leaf or small elements to add to a bead, such as pieces of millefiori or mica.

Knives and Other Cutting Tools

A serrated knife can be used to move glass around on the surface of a bead when you're creating surface designs. For better gripping, use one that has large teeth.

A palette knife, which is a non-serrated knife used by artists for mixing paint on a palette, is excellent for shaping and reaching into narrow places without leaving tool marks behind. You can also use another straight-edged tool, such as a spackling tool or a straight-edged razor in a pin vise from a hardware store.

You can use scissors to cut into the molten glass for shaping purposes. A pair of kitchen shears works well because of its durability. Choose a pair of scissors without plastic parts that are long enough to keep your hands away from the heat while you cut.

Tungsten Picks/Probes

These sharpened heat-resistant tungsten rods with wooden handles are used for various tasks. They are available in straight versions or with the end bent and hooked. They are available in several thicknesses.

Straight picks can be used to make indentations in the glass or rake it. If you preheat this kind of pick, you can use it to pierce a hole in the glass to form a little handle. Picks with a bent, hooked end make raking easier.

Optic Molds

Optic molds made for glass beadmaking are used for the creation of *canes* that are used to decorate beads. The glass is pressed into these metal molds that come in a variety of shapes, such as a heart, moon, or star.

Optic molds are used to create patterned canes.

Support Tools

From the beginning of making a bead until the end, you'll need a set of tools to assist you as you shape the glass. Some of these items actually hold the glass, while others are used to decorate and finish your beads.

Mandrels

Regular mandrels are stainless-steel welding rods used to hold the wound molten glass that forms a bead. They're available in several diameters that range from $3/64$ to $1/8$ inch (1 to 3 mm) and are 9 to 12 inches (22.9 to 30.5 cm) in length. The most common sizes used are $1/16$, $3/32$, and $1/8$ inch (1.6, 2, and 3 mm). The mandrel's diameter determines the size of the bead's hole. Take the bead's design and function into consideration when you choose the diameter you'll use.

Very thin mandrels are easy to accidentally bend when you remove the beads. Do not use a bent mandrel, because if you wind a bead on the bent area, you won't be able to get it off after it cools. If the bent area is close enough to one end of the mandrel, you can clip it off and file the end to remove any barbs that might catch on the bead.

Hollow steel tubing is used to make beads with larger holes. Larger-diameter mandrels, made specifically for creating larger-holed beads, come in a wide variety of sizes. The larger tube-shaped end is welded onto a steel rod that is smaller, allowing you to rotate it easily. Keep in mind that the larger the diameter, the heavier the tool will be, and thus more tiring to use for longer periods of time.

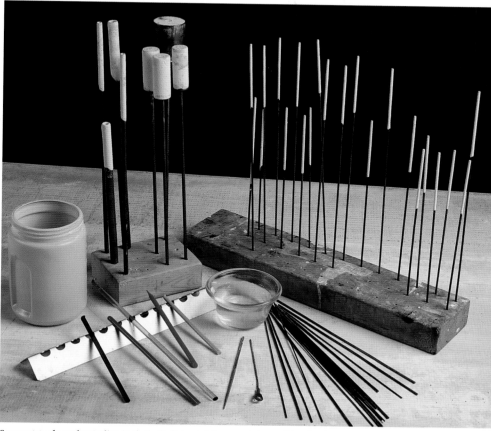

Support tools and supplies include (left to right): a container of bead release, a rod rest, a group of large-hole mandrels in a mandrel block, a quenching bowl, bead reamers, uncoated mandrels, and dipped mandrels in a block

Mandrel Block

Mandrels are dipped in a coating of *bead release* (see page 22) prior to being used, and they must be held upright for even drying. A mandrel block is simply a block of wood with holes drilled into it that supports the uncoated ends of the mandrels. You will probably want to make your own blocks, since it is a simple thing to do, but you can also buy them through beadmaking suppliers.

You'll need separate blocks with different-sized holes for supporting mandrels of various diameters. The holes should be slightly larger than the mandrels they hold. You can

temporarily use a polystyrene block to hold your mandrels, but eventually, you should invest in something more stable.

Rod Rest

A metal rod rest with notches cut in it provides a platform for supporting hot glass rods so that they don't burn the top of your work surface or thermal shock. If you leave the rest in the same place on your workbench, you'll get used to putting the hot glass rods in this safe place, and avoid injuring yourself.

19

You can buy V-shaped rod rests with grooves cut in them for holding the rods. Some beadmakers make their own rod rest from a 10-inch (25.4 cm) length of threaded metal pipe with large bolts attached to each end to keep the pipe from rolling away.

Bead Reamer

After beads have cooled and are removed from the mandrels, you'll have to clean out the holes to remove the excess release. A bead reamer is used for this purpose.

Several versions are available through beadmaking suppliers, including bead reamers that fit into handheld drills as well as small wire brushes that can be used to clean away residue and smooth the inside of your bead. The most commonly used one is a round diamond-encrusted file that helps prevent chips on the rim of the bead's hole if

it doesn't have a well-developed indentation. (You can also use a rod saw blade from a hardware store that has been cut in half lengthwise to clean away the residue.) If you're using mandrels of different sizes, you'll obviously need to think about the size of the reamer that you use.

Punches

Punches, designed for scrapbooking, work very well for punching out shapes of silver or gold foil for decorating the surface of beads.

Tile Nippers

This tool is used to nip or cut glass in either a cold or hot state. Be sure to purchase a pair with tungsten blades. Nippers are available from beadmaking or stained glass suppliers. The ones made for cutting stained glass are preferred by many beadmakers because they have two sharp metal discs that sever the

glass. You can also use a pair of nippers made for cutting tile purchased at a home improvement store.

Glass Crusher

A glass crusher, made of two lengths of capped galvanized pipe that fit together because one is slightly smaller in diameter than the other, is used to crush glass to make *frit*. Short pieces of glass are placed in the bottom of the larger pipe and crushed by slamming the smaller pipe into the larger one. Crushers can be purchased from a glass or beadmaking supplier, or you can make your own.

Sifters

Sifters are used to separate frit, but they also can be used for sprinkling enamel or powders on a bead. They are often used to separate larger pieces of frit from smaller ones. The mesh on sifters varies in size according to their purpose. Smaller-meshed sifters are used for a light application of enamel.

A glass crusher (bottom center) is used to make frit. The two home-made sifters shown here are made from yogurt containers attached to screen mesh. These are used for sizing frit. The small red sifter (center) is used to apply enamel.

Scrapbooking punches make a great tool for punching out shapes of silver or gold foil for decorating beads.

Supplies

Supplies are materials that need to be replaced or restocked on a regular basis. Some supplies, such as enamel or mica powder, are used in very small quantities and won't need to be purchased often. On the other hand, you'll use up glass fairly quickly.

Glass Rod

In its most basic form, glass is a mixture of silica and oxides. This amazing material can be heated to a molten state, altered, and cooled or frozen into a new shape. The proportion of silica to various oxides (soda and lime, borax, or lead) affects its melting temperature and workability while it's molten.

In this book, we'll be working with what is commonly known as *soft glass* (soda lime glass). The name is not an indication of its fragility, or how it behaves in its rigid state. Rather, it describes how quickly the glass heats to the molten state, and its consistency while molten. Since soft glass has a lower melting temperature and is more liquid at this stage, it works well for beadmaking. It is available in a wide palette of colors, since oxides that become altered at the higher melting temperatures needed for borosilicate are not affected at the lower melting temperatures needed for soft glass.

There are several soft glass rods on the market made from different formulas. What's important for you to understand is that you must choose types of glass that are *compatible* when combined. This factor is related to what is known as the *coefficient of expansion* (COE). Each type

Soft glass rods come in a variety of colors, both opaque and transparent.

of glass is given a number to indicate its COE—the degree to which a material expands and contracts at a fixed range of temperature—when heated, brought to molten, or cooled again to a rigid state. Although the COE is scientifically recorded as a long decimal number, it is given a whole number for our purposes.

The COE for soft glass ranges from 89 to 109, while the range for borosilicate is 32 to 33. This difference indicates that soft glass expands and contracts considerably more than hard glass when heated and cooled. For this reason, COE affects how the glass behaves—soft glass can be brought to a molten and workable state more quickly and with less heat than hard glass. For glass to be compatible or "fit," the COE for glass used in beadmaking can't differ by more than a couple of numbers.

Glass is colored by adding metal oxides to clear glass when it is in a molten state. Silver oxide is used to make cream and yellow; cobalt makes blues; copper makes blue-green, green, brown, and various reds; gold makes a beautiful transparent red; and manganese makes purple. In some glass colors, various oxides have been combined to create shading and variation.

The different oxides in each glass color can react with one another in the molten state, depending on how long the glass is worked in the flame. This can create a third color or a dark line between the colors, which can be desirable or not. Some beadmakers use this effect to their advantage (see Appendix A).

Bead Release or Separator

Bead release or separator is a mixture of alumina and high-fire clay used to coat the mandrel so the glass can be removed after it cools. It prevents the glass from sticking to the metal and is available in various strengths, some with more holding power than others.

If you're making beads that have little contact with the mandrel, such as disc-shaped beads, it's good to use a stronger release. You'll have less chance of the bead breaking loose while you're working on it. Similarly, if you're making longer beads, you may want to use a release that is less toothy so that the beads are easier to remove from the mandrels. You may need to try a few different brands before deciding what works for you.

Bead release formulas vary slightly in color, so keep this in mind if you're making transparent beads, since the release can show through the glass. Some brands of release come in a powder form that you mix with water to a thick consistency (similar to pancake batter). Mix and store the release in a tall, narrow container with a snug lid. If you want a really smooth coating, consider dedicating a blender for mixing. If you buy release that is premixed, and it is too thick due to evaporation, simply add some water to it before shaking it up.

The release will separate if it sits for any period of time, so shake it up every time you use it. You can add a small bead to the container to help mix the release when you shake it.

Surface Treatments and Inclusions

In addition to using glass rods, other glass and non-glass materials can be added to your beads to create beautiful, diverse effects. These include ground glass or frit and enamel, or non-glass materials such as metal leaf and finely ground mica.

Frit/Powders

Colored glass that has been crushed or ground into small bits in various grit sizes is known as frit. It was originally made by dumping hot molten glass into cold water to create thermal shock, which would in turn fracture it into small bits. Frit is applied to the surface of the bead to add color and pattern. It is available in various grits. The most commonly used sizes are a larger one similar to sea salt and a smaller one similar to sugar.

Aventurine

Aventurine, first made in Venice in the 15th century, is glass in which oxidized metallic particles are suspended, simulating aventurine quartz, which is a gemstone. The most common is gold aventurine, which has a brilliant brown color and is flecked with copper particles, and green aventurine, where the color is produced with particles of chromium.

If you use this special glass for decorating beads, it has to be compatible with the glass used for your core bead. There are several colors of aventurine that are generally available: gold, dark blue, and green. This glass can be purchased in frit or larger chunks that can be used to make stringers.

Dichroic Glass

Dichroic glass is a beautiful and fascinating glass that changes as it reflects or transmits light. When it's applied to the outside of a bead, it makes it shimmer and shine with a changing pattern of color. This coated glass is made by applying a very thin layer of refractive index materials (aluminum, chromium, silicon, titanium, and zirconium) to various formulas of glass. The glass is created in a heated vacuum chamber, where the materials are applied in various layers and combinations to create different colors. The angle at which dichroic glass is viewed changes the colors.

This glass costs quite a bit more than regular soft glass, and certain colors, such as red, orange, and green, require more layers of material and are more expensive. Soft-glass-compatible dichroic, with a base of either black or clear glass, is available in rod and sheet form. Sheets can be cut into strips before applying them to beads.

Enamel Powder

Enamel powder is a highly pigmented, finely crushed glass with more intense color than frit. Make certain to buy a powder that is compatible with the type of glass you're using. You can increase your surface palette by using enamels. A thin layer can intensify an underlying color or even create a different color. If you sift the powder onto the bead lightly, it will produce a speckled effect.

Examples of surface treatments and inclusions used to decorate beads (counterclockwise from the left): a dish of aventurine frit and bits of chunk, packages of frit and spooned frit, mica powders in tubes, packages of enamel, a large tube of reduction frit, pieces of copper tubing, sheets of gold leaf, and a spool of fine silver wire

Mica Powders

Mica powders (pixie dust) are mica compounds (made up of mica with colorants) in the form of superfine powders. You can use them to lend a pearly luster and metallic effect to beads. They are very sensitive to heat and require delicate application.

Etching Fluid/Cream

After you've cooled a bead, you can etch the surface of it to give it a matt look. Etching fluid or cream can be used for this purpose. The liquid is used to bathe the bead, while the cream can be painted in small areas. Etching cream takes longer to process than liquid fluid.

Metal Leaf/ Foil and Wire

You can transform simple beads with the addition of metal leaf, foil, or wire. Metal foil and leaf create some wonderful effects that can be left on the surface of the bead or cased with transparent glass. Silver, gold, palladium, and copper leaf are sold in books. Foils, which are thicker and more expensive, are sold in individual sheets. On the other hand, foils are easier to handle for cutting into shapes than thin sheets of leaf.

Fine silver wire can also be used for decorating the surface of beads. Very thin wire (such as 28 gauge) works well and can be purchased from jewelry suppliers and some beadmaking suppliers.

Fine Silver Bezel Wire

This thin, flat strip of silver wire is most commonly used in silver-smithing and is available from a jeweler's supplier. For our purposes, we'll be using it to prepare a rod for fuming (see page 119). It is heated at the torch and melted onto a borosilicate or quartz glass rod. Be sure to purchase fine silver bezel, since sterling contains other metals that can conflict with the fuming technique.

Copper Tubing

Copper tubing is used in beadmaking as a decorative base for beads. The tubing turns a beautiful bright copper color when you apply heat to it. After a short piece of it is slipped over a mandrel, you can wrap molten glass directly on it. Using a light transparent glass color over the tubing creates a stunning effect.

Cut tubing can be purchased from some beadmaking suppliers in lengths ranging from $1/2$ to 2 inches (1.3 to 5 cm). You can also buy a length of tubing from a home improvement store, and cut it yourself or have it cut for you.

Mass-Produced Cane or Millefiori

Remember those lovely glass paperweights with colorful, complex flower shapes inside of them? They're made with an ancient Italian glass technique. Millefiori canes are made by bundling several glass rods together to create a patterned cross-section that is sliced to show the design. These canes are actually made from a very large layered or shaped design that is heated and pulled out into a smaller version of the original design.

There are many different kinds of millefiori available in soft glass that can be used for bead surface decoration. Some canes have an image or design in the cross-section only, while others have a decorative border around the design on the outside (usually stripes).

The canes are usually presliced. A thinner slice of about $1/8$ inch (3 mm) or less in length is ideal for cane with an interior design that you plan to apply to a bead. A slightly thicker slice works better for cane with a design on the outside as well as the inside. (In chapter 5 you'll learn how to make your own millefiori.)

Safety Equipment and Clothing

Since you're working with fire and molten glass when you make beads, it's imperative that you think about safety every step of the way. This section introduces you to the equipment and clothing that protect you from burns and respiratory problems.

Protective Lenses

When working with glass and a flame, it's vital to protect your eyes from possible glass shards that can fly off if you put a rod into the flame too quickly. If you begin working with a single-fuel torch, the flame is large and bushy, without clearly defined edges. It's important to be able to see all regions of it clearly while you learn where they are. For this reason, we suggest that you not use filtered glasses in the beginning, but use protective clear or minimally shaded shop glasses while you learn.

Once you've become accustomed to the flame, and know instinctively where the regions are, wear safety glasses from a beadmaking supplier made of didymium or another alternate lens material that blocks the bright yellow light ("sodium flare") emitted by glass in the flame.

These glasses not only help you see what you're doing better but give you some protection against potentially harmful rays. They are particularly important to wear when working with a dual-fuel torch, since it emits more heat and a brighter flare. Your proximity to the hot, glowing glass affects your

You'll need to keep and use various safety items in your studio including a fire extinguisher, protective lenses, and gloves.

exposure. Some experts suggest that staying around 10 inches (25.4 cm) away from the flame used for working with soft glass will provide adequate protection against infrared and ultraviolet rays.

If you're doing a lot of detail work and need to hold the work close, you may want to consider additional lens protection, such as lenses with a reflective coating on the outside. You can also wear clip-on welder's shades over your other lenses. These glasses are quite dark, however, and make it more difficult for you to see colors well.

As you spend more time at the torch, do your own research about eye protection so that you know the most up-to-date lens technology. If you plan to work a lot,

it's worth knowing about the best possible protection currently available to you.

If you end up doing a lot of fuming as a part of your work, be sure to wear extra protection (such as welder's clip-on glasses), since this process creates a very bright flare that requires extra filtering.

Gloves

Wear protective gloves when you're working with a heated kiln, for instance, when you put beads inside to anneal. Even though you'll be sticking your hand in and out quickly, the heat of a kiln at annealing temperature (approximately 970°F or 521°C) is too hot for unprotected skin.

Clothing

To prevent burns, you must also pay attention to the clothing you wear in your studio. Wear clothing made of natural fibers such as cotton or linen rather than synthetic clothing, such as nylon or polyester, since these can melt if overheated.

Cover as much of your skin as possible with long pants, long sleeves, and high-necked tops. Remember that exposed areas are susceptible to hot bits of glass that might pop out of the fire from the end of a rod. Avoid long sleeves that are open at the wrist, pocketed shirts and cuffed pants (because they might hold a hot bit of glass if it pops off), and open shoes or sandals. Keep your hair pulled or tied back from your face.

First-Aid Kit

When you're working with hot molten glass, burns are almost impossible to avoid. Always have a first-aid kit close at hand containing burn cream and bandages. If you have a minor burn, you can cool it with water (not ice), and bandage it if needed. Aloe gel from a tube or a live plant in your studio is also handy for soothing minor burns. Since silver draws heat, you can also use a silver ring or spoon to cool the burn if you hold it against your skin.

If you end up with a chemical burn, such as one that you might get if you splatter etching fluid on your skin, follow the manufacturer's recommendations on the bottle.

Fire Extinguisher

Always keep at least one fire extinguisher in your studio that you can reach from the torch if a fire happens suddenly. Keep another one in a separate location in your studio for extra safety. It's a good idea to check with your local fire department or fire marshal about the correct size and type of extinguisher.

Check the pressure on each of them regularly to be sure they'll function in an emergency. An ABC type fire extinguisher utilizes a non-toxic dry chemical agent and is highly effective on combustibles, oils or chemicals, and electrical fires.

Leak Detection Fluid

Use this fluid to make sure that all the connections that carry oxygen or propane from the tanks to the torch are snug. Available from an oxygen or beadmaking supplier, this sprayed-on liquid bubbles up if a gas leak is present between connections (see page 12 for more information about using this fluid).

Glass Disposal Containers

You'll need a fireproof container, such as a large tin can or a small galvanized bucket from a home improvement store, for the safe disposal of hot bits of glass while working at the torch. When this bucket is full, you'll empty the glass into a galvanized metal garbage can. This can is designated for glass only—NEVER place anything combustible in it, such as paper.

NOTE

If fire erupts and gets close to your pressurized gas tanks, you should evacuate your studio immediately and call the fire department!

Carbon Monoxide Detector

Carbon monoxide is an invisible and odorless poisonous gas produced by incomplete combustion of any torch fuel. Therefore, it's very important to mount a carbon monoxide (CO) detector in your studio, since this gas can accumulate while you're working and is not noticeable. It is also of utmost importance to have a good ventilation system, as discussed on page 27.

Mount the detector close to where you sit at the torch. If you're using a battery-charged detector rather than a plug-in electric one, be sure that the battery is fully charged.

High concentrations of carbon monoxide can be very dangerous to your health. Headaches, drowsiness, fatigue, or nausea can indicate CO exposure. If you experience such symptoms while working, leave your studio and get fresh air. If your symptoms don't decrease, you should seek medical attention.

Quenching Bowl

Keep a heat-resistant glass bowl with water in it on your work surface for cooling off your metal tools. You can also remove unwanted glass from the end of a rod, stringer, or tool by chilling it quickly in the water to thermal shock it so that it drops off into the water.

Setting Up and Working in Your Studio

Setting up a studio requires a bit of work, but it is not terribly complicated or expensive, and it doesn't require a lot of space. The only size consideration for your space is that it be large enough that the torch doesn't face a wall or corner. Choose a location for your workspace that's easy to evacuate in case of a fire.

The space should contain as little combustible material in it as possible. The floor beneath work areas must be flameproof. A concrete floor is ideal. Or, you can cover your floor with nonflammable, nonporous material such as cement board (used for backing tile in bathrooms), ceramic tile, slate, or stainless steel. You must also cover your workbench (table) with a nonflammable material.

In the section that follows, you'll learn about ventilation, setting up an exhaust system, lighting, and ergonomics—important topics that affect your ability to work safely and comfortably in your studio.

Ventilating Your Studio Properly

Melting glass in a flame results in a number of gases and vapors that can affect your health. Therefore, *never* underestimate the importance of ventilating your work area. At the very least, you must have ventilation that creates a steady flow of air across your work area, drawing vapors and gases away from your face and out of the room.

If you're a beginner, you can make do with an exhaust fan on one end of your work area and a regular fan on the other to bring in fresh air, diluting noxious fumes. In any case, you need to make sure that you're not only drawing the air out of the space, but replacing it as well. Don't create a strong breeze, however, since this will interfere with the torch flame and can cause the glass to shock.

Exhaust System

If you plan to make beads on a regular basis for sustained periods of time, install a more sophisticated ventilation system, which is usually composed of a hood positioned over your torch that is attached to ductwork with an exhaust fan at the end.

Ideally, the hood should be about 4 feet (1.2 m) long and wide, with the majority of it positioned in front of the torch to collect any noxious fumes. Locate the exhaust so that it goes outside to an area that is far away from the place where you draw in fresh air. You can buy a metal exhaust hood (like the ones made for ranges), or you can make one yourself (see below). On the Internet, you can also find bead-making suppliers who make hoods just for this purpose. Find one in your geographic area so that you can transport the hood.

When you set up any ventilation system (whether purchased or made) consult with an air or safety specialist about your setup to make sure that you've set it up properly and it exhausts safely.

MAKING YOUR OWN EXHAUST SYSTEM: In my studio, I use an exhaust system connected to ducting that leads to a laundry vent with a flap that opens out with the flow of air. The exhaust fan is at the far end of the ducting near the outside wall where

> **NOTE**
>
> *As you work in your studio and air quality decreases, you might not be aware of it. If you have any signs of exposure to fumes, such as a metallic taste in your mouth, headaches, shortness of breath, or anything else out of the ordinary, it may mean that you have inadequate ventilation.*

the laundry vent is. This creates a vacuum effect in the duct. Avoid severe twists or turns in the ducting to avoid interrupting the flow of air.

Since it might be difficult to find an exhaust hood in a size that you like, you might choose to make your own. You can make one from thermal-resistant insulation board made of polyisocyanurate (polyiso for short) with white foil on one side and silver on the other. This fibrous, virtually non-flammable material usually comes in 4 x 8 foot (1.2 x 2.4 m) sheets. (See Appendix B for instructions.)

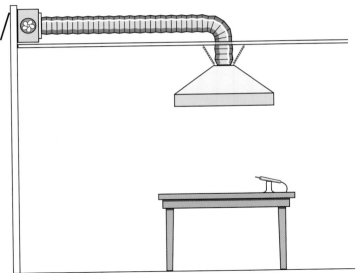

You can make your own exhaust hood and system for your studio using materials that are available from a home improvement store.

Setting Up Your Workbench

You'll need a sturdy table or tables (workbench) for holding your torch, tools, glass, and any other equipment. You can make your own or have one built that suits your needs. An L-shaped configuration of two tables expands the amount of the reachable surface.

The workbench should be tall enough that you can stand or sit at it. (If you are using ready-made tables, you can elevate the legs on wood blocks, but make sure that the legs are bolted to the blocks so that the table is stable.) Being able to stand up will give your back relief from always sitting in one position.

As mentioned in the safety section, cover the top of the table with flameproof material. You can use cement board, which is a material commonly used for flooring underneath tiles or slate. It is made from cement with a fibrous

support structure. Mark the size you need for your table, score it with a utility knife, and then break it along the lines.

You can also use stainless or galvanized steel as your work surface on top of your table. Be sure to purchase sheet metal thick enough that it won't warp from occasional exposure to molten glass. Even though it's more expensive than cement board, it's much easier to clean. Contact a local sheet metal contractor to get a top made that fits your table.

Use a chair that can be adjusted easily for height and has back support. The design of it should be such that you can easily get out of it in case hot glass lands in your lap.

Lighting Your Studio

Since you'll be working with a bright flame in beadmaking, your lighting setup is very important. Consider investing in full-spectrum overhead lighting. It is more expensive than ordinary fluorescents, but consumes much less electricity.

Unfortunately, ordinary cool white fluorescent lighting that most of us are accustomed to provides unbalanced spectral distribution, and throws a greenish, yellowish hue on a room, distorting colors. Full-spectrum flourescent overhead lighting, that simulates daylight, is the ideal lighting source, because it is not only diffused and even, but doesn't alter the color of the glass.

Daylight is the best light source because you'll be able to see the color at its truest. If you are lucky enough to have windows in your studio, use the available light during the day by hanging window shades that diffuse it.

Ergonomics

Working with hot glass, like any other repetitive motion endeavor, can cause difficulties. The following tips will help you avoid strain as you spend hours at the torch.

❧ Vary your position regularly. If you stay in the same position all the time, you'll put stress on your neck, back, arms, and hands.

❧ Extended sitting can lead to stress on your lower back. Therefore, use a table of a height that allows you to both sit and stand. (If you need to adapt a shorter table, you can elevate it with wood blocks.)

❧ An adjustable chair allows you to vary your position up and down—another way to avoid stressing your arms, back, and neck. The chair should also have a supportive back.

❧ Holding your hands in front of you at chest level or higher without support is also stressful on the back. Position yourself so that you can rest your arms against the edge of the table as well as on the table. (Keep this in mind if you're having a table built!)

Armrests can be used to support your arms while working.

❧ Armrests for supporting your arms can give you a needed break. These are available through some beadmaking suppliers. Avoid positioning your arms too high, since this will create more stress on your back and shoulders. Since the armrests aren't adjustable, you must adjust the height of your chair or table until your arms are resting in a comfortable position.

❧ Position yourself so that you don't have to lean your head too far forward, avoiding strain on your neck and back. Your head is a heavy appendage and, whether you realize it or not, it takes a lot of strength to hold it up. If you have to lean your head forward or down, you probably need to reposition your setup.

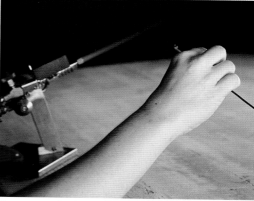

Keep your wrists in a neutral or straight position to reduce stress on your wrists and fingers.

❧ Watch the position of your hands, and try to vary them as well. Do your best to hold your hands with your wrists in a neutral (or straight) position, as shown above. This takes some practice, and can be difficult while holding a mandrel and winding a bead. If you begin to feel tingling and numbness in your fingers, take a good look at your position of wrists and elbows.

❧ Stand up from the torch and move every 30 minutes or so. Stretch, touch your toes, and get a little more blood flowing. Maintaining one position (especially a sitting one) for a long time is stressful on the body.

Making the First Bead

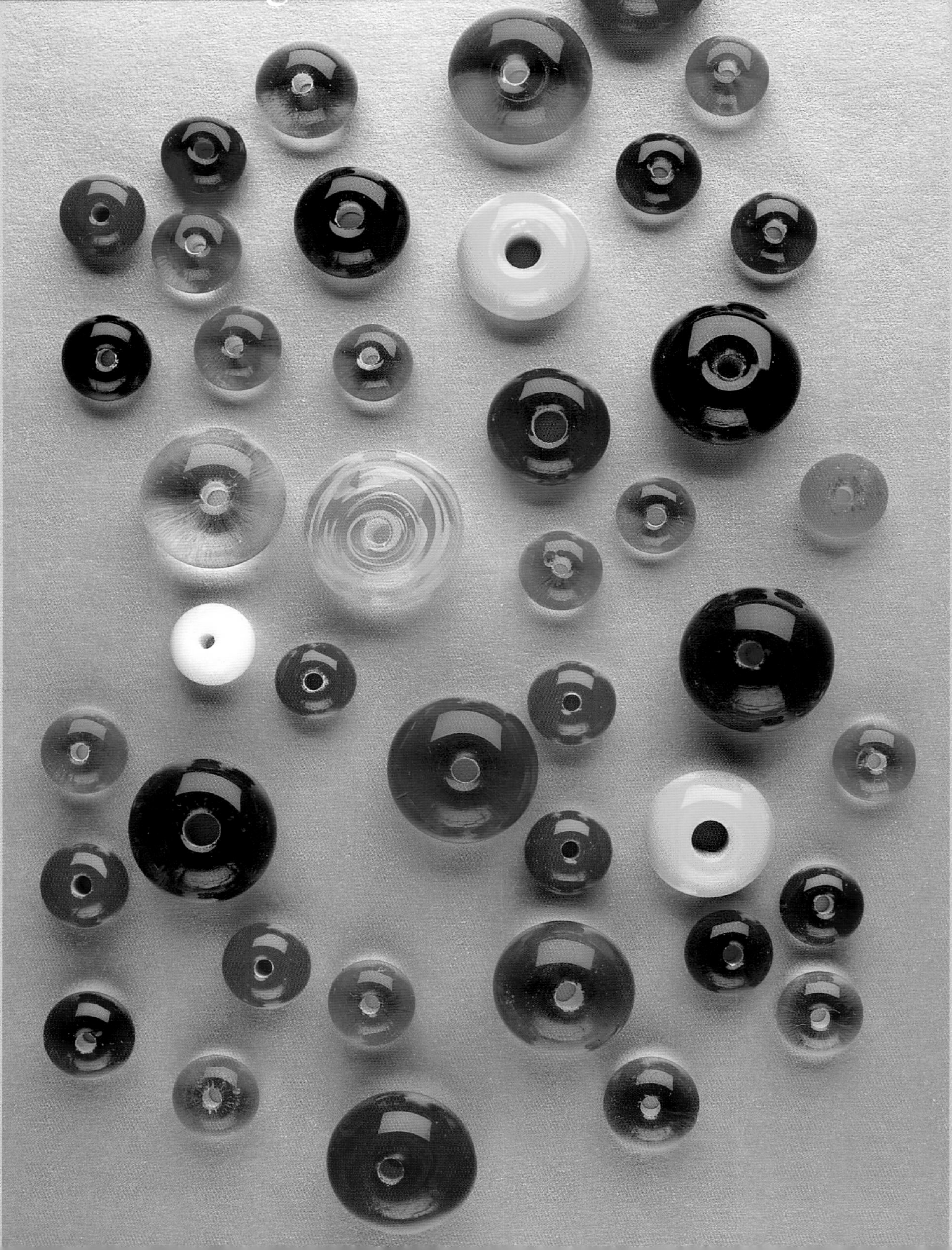

This chapter shows you how to make simple beads with no decoration—the basis for every bead that you'll make. This can be both exciting and challenging. Keep in mind that nobody has made a perfect bead the first time, and that you'll eventually be in sync with the flow of the molten glass so that you can control it.

In essence, you'll heat the glass rod until it is molten before transferring it to the mandrel to form a bead. Practice this beginning step over and over until you can do it consistently, before moving on to the next phase of beadmaking.

Prepping the Mandrels

Before making a glass bead, you'll need to prepare the mandrels. Start by making sure that each mandrel is clean and straight (with no bends in it). Then dip each one down into a container of prepared bead release, covering about 3 inches (7.6 cm). Pull it out, being careful not to bump the side of the container (photo 1). Make sure that each has a consistent layer of release. If part of the metal is showing or not evenly covered, dip it again.

To give yourself an alternative way to work on a mandrel, coat the center of it. To do this, dip it well past its midpoint. Then, use your hands to strip off enough of the release from the mandrel's end, leaving the center section covered so that you can wrap a bead there (photo 2). Coating the middle allows you to hold the mandrel from either end. You'll be able to flip the mandrel and bead over so that you can use your dominant hand to work on each end of the bead. If you use this technique, keep the ends of the mandrel out of the flame so they don't get too hot to touch.

After coating the mandrels, position them upright in a block (see page 19) so that the coating will stay even and unmarred. Dip several mandrels at once so you don't have to stop in the middle of making beads to prepare them. Allow time for them to dry (if you aren't using a flame-dry formula). You can speed up this time by placing the rods in a sunny spot, beside a light source, next to a fan, or on top of a preheated kiln.

If you use a flame-dry formula, make sure to dry all of the release, not just the area where you'll wrap the bead. Any moisture that isn't removed can cause bubbles later on in molten glass.

Lighting the Torch

Working with a torch and gas-fueled flame can seem slightly intimidating at first, but the next section will help you understand the process of lighting the torch, adjusting the flame, and turning it off. Read the instructions thoroughly before you attempt this process. Work with the flame until you feel comfortable with it before you heat up your first rod of glass.

Using a Single-Fuel Torch

If you're learning to use a single-fuel torch, you'll begin by practicing how to open and close the torch valve. When you open the valve, the gas will create a rushing noise. Use a striker to light this type of torch, since the force of the gas can blow out a match or lighter.

With your striker handy, turn the valve slowly counterclockwise (left) until you hear a low rushing sound and gas starts to flow. Hold the striker close to the tip of the torch and light the gas by creating a spark with the striker. If the gas won't light with the first few strikes, turn the valve slightly to open it more and allow more gas to flow. If the flame lights and then goes out, repeat this again, allowing a bit more gas to flow. You might have to practice this several times to get the torch to light easily and consistently.

Once the flame is lit, adjust the torch valve until there's a sharp, cone-shaped blue flame coming directly from the tip of the torch (photo 1). Adjust the flow of the gas so that the cone is about 1 inch (2.5 cm) long and there is no yellow in the flame. If the flame has any turquoise in it, the torch is turned up too high.

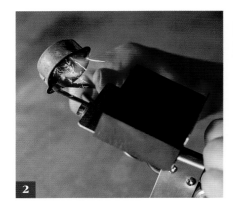

To turn off this type of torch, turn the valve on the torch head to the right until the flame extinguishes completely. Don't wrench the valve closed, since this will deteriorate the valve's inner workings, but do make sure that the flame is out.

Using a Dual-Fuel Torch

On an oxygen/propane torch, practice opening both valves on the torch separately. The top valve, usually red, opens the flow of propane. Since the propane flow has such a low psi, you won't hear any noise when you open the valve. The oxygen valve, often green or unpainted, is usually located on the side of the torch, and you'll turn it toward yourself and over the top. When you open this valve, you'll hear a low hissing sound.

To begin the process of lighting the torch, turn the propane valve counterclockwise about a quarter of the way before using a striker or match to light the propane at the tip of the torch (photo 2). Open the propane valve further so that the flame is 7 to 8 inches (17.8 to 20.3 cm) long (photo 3, next page).

Next, open the oxygen valve about a quarter of the way to establish

the flow, turning it toward you. The psi for the oxygen might need to be readjusted at the regulator (see page 12). Continue to turn the oxygen valve toward you, adjusting the flame until the ring of cones at the tip of the torch shrinks to about $3/8$ inch (9.5 mm) and is defined well (photos 4, 5, and 6). As long as the torch is lighted, you'll hear a low and airy rushing sound.

To turn off this type of torch, close the oxygen valve by turning it away from yourself to stop the flow, without over-tightening it. One indication that this is done is the lack of a bluish-white glow at the tip of the

torch. To turn off the propane, turn the valve to the right, and make certain that the flame is out. As usual, don't over-tighten the valve.

NOTE

If you're using a dual-fuel (oxygen/propane) torch, you can use the letters P-O-O-P to remind you of the order that you need to turn the gases on and off. When you're lighting the torch, you should turn on propane before oxygen. When you're extinguishing the torch, do the opposite—turn the oxygen off first, and then the propane.

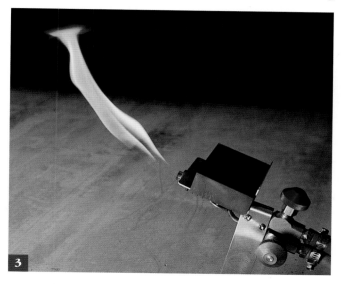

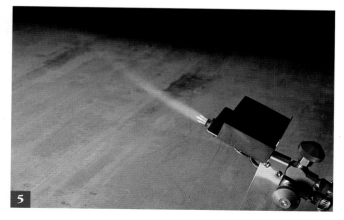

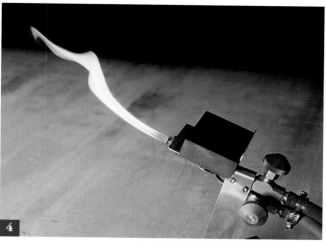

Heating Glass in the Flame

Heating glass in the flame and controlling it as it softens to molten takes practice and patience. Although gravity gives you the ability to shape this molten material, the pull of it will also provide you with plenty of challenges. Your best teacher is trial-and-error, but the following section will give you the basics and great tips about how to make this process work more smoothly. As you work at it, you'll learn to think ahead and adjust your positioning as you move the bead in and out of the flame.

Eventually, you won't have to think about what you are doing, and shaping a mass of glass into a bead will come naturally to you. Enjoy this part of the learning process—shaping your first beads can be exciting if you allow yourself to play at it instead of taking it too seriously.

Regions of the Flame

The flame on a torch varies in temperature from one end to the other. These areas of differing temperature are divided into regions, which we have numbered for easy reference. Understanding these will help you gauge what you're doing. Before you begin any serious work, you should be able to recognize them, since they're elemental to

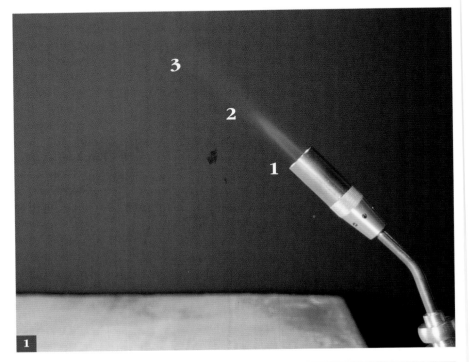

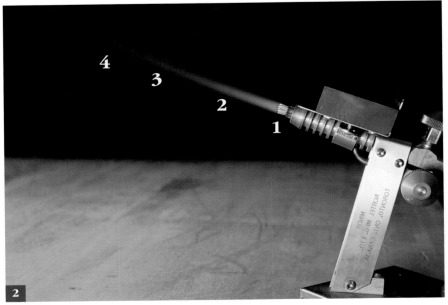

heating and cooling glass when making beads.

A single-fuel (brazing fuel) flame has a blue cone at the tip (as previously described) that you can monitor to make sure that the flame's size is adjusted correctly, indicating the right mixture of heat and oxygen. This area is designated as the first region on this type of torch. *Do not* use this area to heat glass, since it will burn your glass.

The second region, which is located about 1 inch (2.5 cm) from the tip of the blue cone, is the best spot for heating and melting the glass. It has a good mixture of oxygen and brazing fuel, allowing glass to melt without burning it.

Further out, and less visible, is the end of the flame. This third region is still hot, but not enough to melt glass. Study photo 1 to acquaint yourself with these regions.

The dual-fuel torch has shorter regions that are closer to the tip of the torch. The ring of cones in the first region at the tip of the torch doesn't contain the right mix of oxygen and propane and, as a result, will burn the glass. Also, if you get this close to this type of torch with hot glass, you might drop it into the torch tip and block the orifices.

On this type of torch, the best area to use for melting glass is the second region, located about 1½ inches (3.8 cm) away from the cones. At this point, the fuels are mixed well. As you work your way out in the flame into regions three and four, there is less and less heat. You can keep beads warm in region four where it won't melt. Study photo 2 to acquaint yourself with these regions.

Heating Glass to a Molten State

In the following section, you'll learn how to safely heat glass and avoid thermal shock, you'll begin to effectively read the heat of the glass, and you'll learn about the ever-present pull of gravity on molten glass and how it affects what you're doing.

To begin working with glass at the torch, hold the rod like a pencil in your dominant hand, bent toward the flame at an angle. Place the tip of the rod in the end of the flame (photo 3) and move it in and out a few times to warm it up. Then hold the rod steady while you heat about ¼ inch (6 mm) of it. If bits

of glass pop off the rod's end, move the tip of the rod further out into the cooler part of the flame. Wait for the end of the rod to barely glow orange. Allow this orange glow to grow slightly, and then move the rod into a hotter region.

Now heat about ½ inch (1.3 cm) of the glass rod at the tip. Use your fingers to begin rotating the rod as the glass heats and begins to slump, staying ahead of gravity and keeping the glass centered. Move the rod to a horizontal position, and continue to heat and rotate it as the tip of the rod begins to soften, droop, and round off (photo 4).

3

4

Continue to turn the rod in the flame and keep the molten glass aligned with the rod to prevent the glass from drooping. This action keeps it from elongating and getting out of control. Keep practicing this process of heating and controlling the molten glass until it comes naturally. It is very important to master this step.

If the glass becomes so molten that it begins to get out of control, bring it of the flame. When the glass is removed, it will immediately begin to cool and stiffen, making it easier to work with. You can also move out to a cooler part of the flame if the glass gets too hot.

Winding the First Bead

After you've learned to control the glass in the flame, you'll be able to wrap it around a mandrel to create a basic bead. The illustrated steps that follow will help you understand this process. Give yourself time as you do this, and try to learn from your mistakes. Practice will be your best teacher.

While you are learning to work with the glass, one of the most important steps is heating the glass to molten. You'll become aware of the importance of "reading the heat" of the bead. Throughout the text of this book, we'll use color descriptions to describe how the bead looks when it's reached the right temperature for a particular stage of beadmaking. Descriptions such as dull orange, bright orange, and red glow will assist you as you learn to read the heat. The brighter the glow from the glass, the hotter and more molten is. As the glow begins to fade, this indicates that the glass is cooling and firming up. Eventually, the glow will be completely gone, and it will be rigid. The more time you spend working with glass in its molten state, the better you'll become at reading the heat and knowing when it's the right temperature to do whatever it is that you need to do.

The Steps

To make your first bead, begin by learning how to hold a coated mandrel properly. Hold it in your non-dominant hand in an overhand position, using your little finger as a balancing point. Use your first finger and thumb to turn it up, over, and away from you (photo 1). Hold the mandrel steady and horizontal as you turn it, and don't let it wobble.

Next, heat about ¹/₂ inch (1.3 cm) of glass in the flame in your dominant hand. Start in the coolest part of it. As the glass warms and begins to glow orange, move up to the hotter part of the flame (between the sec-ond and third region) and continue to heat the glass until it is molten.

Meanwhile, the mandrel should be hot enough for the glass to stick to it. So, as you move the glass into the hotter part of the flame, place the mandrel in the cooler part and heat a spot about 1 inch (2.5 cm) from the end of it. Use your non-dominant hand to hold it. Rotate it back and forth a few times, heating it to an orange glow (photo 2).

As the glass becomes molten and glows bright orange, bring the cool end of the rod around toward you, with the hot end pointing down into the flame at a 90° angle to the man-drel. Rotate the mandrel up and away from you, while lightly touching the molten glass down on the preheated area. Pull the molten glass off the rod and onto the mandrel, continuing to rotate the mandrel in the same direction (photo 3).

Drop the mandrel slightly below the flame in a horizontal position, holding the glass rod so that it points down through the flame.

> ## NOTE
>
> *It is possible to overheat the mandrel and melt the metal, so bring it out of the flame immediately if it gets really bright or begins to spark. Start over with a new mandrel, since overheating causes the metal to expand and makes it unusable. You can nip off the melted area after the mandrel cools, and use it again.*

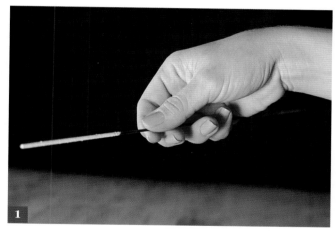

1

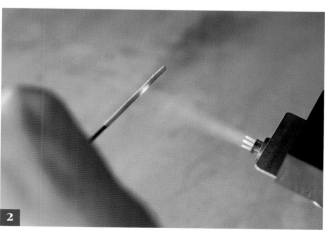

2

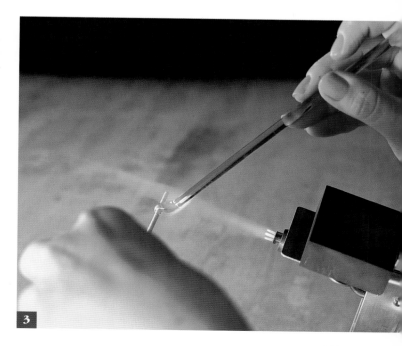

3

As more glass heats and becomes molten, continue to rotate the mandrel, gently pulling the molten glass off onto it. Position the glass and mandrel so that the flame is aimed at the rod just above the connection between it and the newly formed bead (photo 4).

Be careful to pull off only the molten part of the glass as you work—it should be molten enough to pull off the rod easily. If not, it will be stiff and won't wind

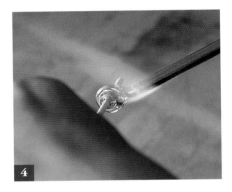

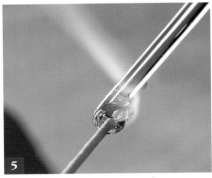

properly (photo 5). Trying to force it can loosen the bead. If the release breaks loose, start over with a newly coated mandrel and glass without residual release on it. If you have release on the rod, melt it and pull it off with tweezers. Drop it in your quenching bowl.

Continue to build up glass until the bead is the size of a marble. As you do this, hold the rod of glass in one place without moving it up or down on the mandrel. Always maintain the mandrel's horizontal position while working.

To separate the rod from the bead, lift the glass rod about $^1/_2$ inch (1.3 cm) away from the bead. Keep rotating the mandrel up, over, and away from you, so that the molten rod separates naturally from the bead in the flame. The connections between the rod and the bead will get thinner and thinner until it parts cleanly and completely (photo 6). This technique is known as

flame-cutting. When you do this, be certain that the molten glass is completely separated before bringing the rod out of the flame, or you'll end up with a hair-like thread of glass between the bead and rod.

Once the glass rod and bead are separated, place the rod on the rod rest on your workbench with the hot end elevated. Move the bead out in the flame so it's about $2^1/_2$ inches (6.4 cm) from the cone(s). Continue to heat and turn the bead, allowing the glass to become very molten and a bright glowing orange color. Allow the molten glass to round off and smooth out (photo 7) while you keep turning the bead.

Take the bead out of the flame, and continue to rotate it to counteract gravity. As you do this, hold the mandrel horizontally so that gravity doesn't pull the bead out of shape to the left or right. If the bead is uneven, pause in each rotation with the heavy side on top, allowing gravity to pull the molten glass down (photo 8). Doing this will make the bead more symmetrical or "round it up." Pause only for a second, and then turn it again while taking a look at the shape of the bead. You might need to reheat it and do this again several times before it's symmetrical.

Varying the Bead's Shape

You've already learned quite a bit about gravity through winding your first bead. As you rotated the mandrel to keep the bead on center, you did the simplest kind of shaping. As you've probably already discovered, gravity is a force that can quickly pull a bead out of shape if you don't work with it properly. This force will cause the molten glass to sag as soon as you stop rotating the bead. However, this factor is exactly why you'll be able to make various shapes, such as teardrop or asymmetrical forms.

To form a simple teardrop bead, start with a round bead. Stop

rotating the mandrel and point it up or down. The glass will flow and form a teardrop shape. Don't allow the thin end of the bead to become too thin, since it's more likely to chip once it's removed from the mandrel (photo 1).

To make a long bead, wind the glass up and down the mandrel and overlap it as desired. Add glass so that the shape is slightly narrower and taller than your final bead with a little extra glass built up at the ends. Be sure the bead is symmetrical around the mandrel.

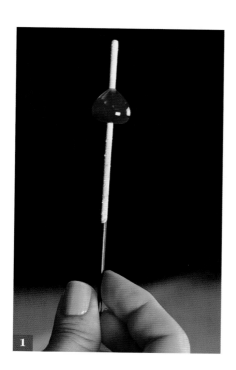

Finishing Up the Ends of Beads

A nicely made bead has well-formed ends that are slightly rounded and indented (photo 2). It's important that the edge of the bead's hole be slightly rounded rather than sharp, since the edge can chip or potentially cut the material on which the bead is strung. You can achieve this effect by using gravity to thicken up the ends so that each is indented, or you can roll and press the bead on a marver.

Gravity

Let's start with finishing off the ends of a round bead. Build up the molten glass so that it's taller than the bead that you'd like to end up making (photo 3). Aim the flame at an angle at the top of the bead, with the mandrel held horizontal, slightly below the flame.

Heat the glass until it glows bright orange, continuously turning it in a horizontal position to maintain its symmetrical shape. As it softens, the glass will begin to flow outward, lengthening the bead slightly and creating a small indentation at each end of the bead (photo 4). Bring it out of the flame, still

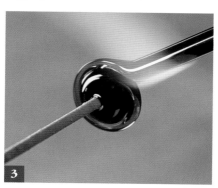

turning it while you hold it horizontal. Check for good indentations when you bring it out of the flame.

To make indentations on a long bead, be sure the bead is symmetrical around the mandrel. Work on one end of the bead at a time, turning it in the flame until it glows bright orange. Hold the mandrel at an angle so that the glass flows toward the molten end of the

bead (photo 5). Continue turning the bead. Keep an eye on the glass as it flows and creates an indentation.

Then, bring the bead out of the flame and check the indentation, still turning it at an angle and letting the glass cool until it no longer glows and the glass is rigid. Move to the other end of the bead and repeat the process (photo 6).

Marver Method

You can also roll a molten bead on a marver or paddle to push the glass out toward the ends. Roll the bead with light pressure so that a small amount of glass is pushed toward the ends of it, and it bulges slightly over the glass surrounding the mandrel. Begin with very light pressure, and increase it as the glass cools and firms up.

If you're working on a round bead, roll it parallel to the marver, moving the molten glass out to both ends simultaneously (photo 7). On a longer bead, work on each end separately. Heat one end of the bead, and roll it lightly on the marver until the indentation forms. Then move to the opposite end of the bead and repeat this process.

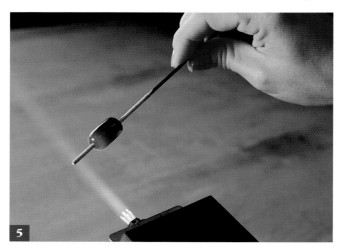

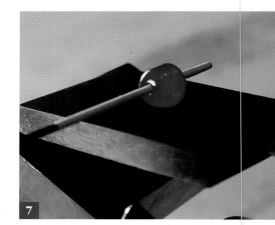

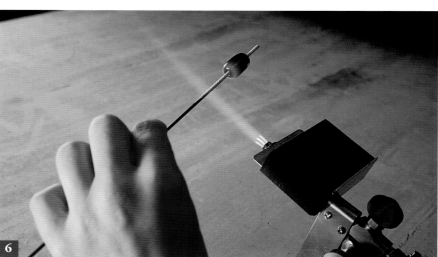

Flame Annealing and Cooling

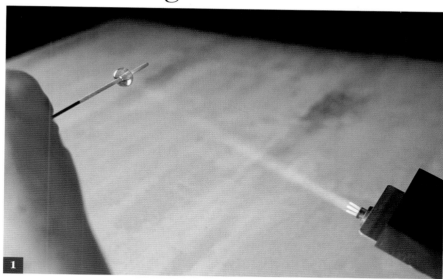

NOTE

Always extinguish the torch if you don't plan to make any more beads or won't be attending to it, even if only for a brief moment or two. Never leave the flame unattended.

When you're satisfied with the shape of the bead, move it out to the tip of the flame to gradually cool it. Continue to rotate the bead, since gravity can still pull it out of shape. The glow will fade from bright orange to a low red glow as the glass cools and gets rigid (photo 1).

This step, called *flame annealing*, is an important part of beadmaking. It helps even out the temperature throughout the bead, and slows the cooling of the glass while the temperature drops from molten at 1700°F (927°C) to rigid at roughly 970°F (521°C). It helps prevent thermal shock that leads to your glass breaking.

To flame-anneal a bead with a single-fuel torch, keep it in the tip of the flame until the bead changes to an even dull red glow. The tip of this flame is cool enough to allow the glass to return to its rigid state. At this point, remove it from the flame and allow the glow to fade.

If you're using a dual-fuel torch, move the bead to the coolest part of the flame (out in the tip of it) until the bead is evenly heated to a dull red glow. (Depending on the complexity and size of the bead, some sections of it may be much hotter than others. It's important that the bead has an even glow with no bright orange or very dark areas.) Quickly take the bead out of the flame, turn off the oxygen, and return the bead to the propane-only flame until the glow is completely gone (photo 2).

After the glow has left the bead, you must slow the cooling of it more to prevent thermal shock. If you're not ready to anneal your bead in the kiln, you can do this by placing it between two layers of ceramic fiber blanket or in a pre-heated crock-pot filled with vermiculite. If you're using a fiber blanket, don't disturb the beads until they cool to room temperature. The beads will cool in about 20 to 30 minutes, depending on how many beads are in the blanket and their size. In the case of vermiculite, leave the beads in the heated substance for about 45 minutes before moving them to a room-temperature container filled with vermiculite. Let the beads cool completely.

If you're making several beads, you can cool and anneal them in a preheated kiln, right after flame annealing. If you're using any of these cooling methods, make sure that the beads don't touch one another, since this can lead to thermal shock.

Annealing in the Kiln

As discussed before, you can temporarily cool your beads in a fiber blanket or vermiculite after flame annealing. You can even remove them from their mandrels and clean them (see page 43) without breaking them. However, stress will not be completely relieved until you anneal your beads in the kiln. For your beads to be completely finished, and not susceptible to breaking, you must anneal them in a kiln.

In general, the process of annealing is used to render various materials less brittle by releasing internal stresses through gradual cooling. In glass, this is achieved in a kiln, where the temperature can be controlled and dropped slowly. The end result is a molecular alignment with little or no stress.

To understand the whole cycle of heating and cooling glass, it is helpful to know what happens when it is taken from room temperature to molten. When heat is applied, the molecules in glass begin vibrating, breaking the bonds between them. As the temperature increases, more bonds are broken until the glass is molten. During this process, it expands.

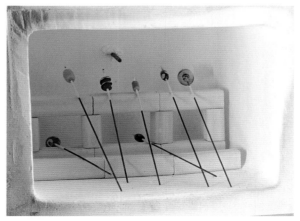

As the glass cools and returns to the rigid state, the molecular vibrations slow down. If this happens too quickly, the molecules align improperly and stress is created. To relieve the stress, the glass has to be held at a steady temperature in the kiln long enough to remove all stress and cool down evenly so that all the molecules slow down at essentially the same rate, allowing them to line up properly. In relation to this, the outside of the bead will then cool at the same rate as the inside.

There are several soft glass formulas and each has a slightly different COE, giving each glass a different *annealing temperature*—the temperature at which the molecules vibrate enough to relieve stress in the glass over a period of time without being too hot to flow. The annealing temperature for the soft glass demonstrated in this book is about 970°F (521°C). This is the temperature at which a bead (outside and inside, as well as thicker and thinner parts) should be held, or soaked, at a steady temperature over a length of time. For most glass beads, the soaking time is 15 to 30 minutes, although very large beads require a bit more time.

The amount of surface area on a bead affects its cooling rate and thus the time needed to soak it. This comes into play if you're making beads with added details such as handles, wings, or other extensions. These thinner portions of the bead with more surface area will cool more quickly than the base. These beads should be soaked longer and cooled more slowly, allowing the thinner portions to cool at the same rate as thicker portions.

After the beads have soaked for the appropriate time, you'll allow the temperature to drop in the kiln. If you're using a larger or brick-lined kiln, you can usually just turn it off, since the size of it holds heat well and cools slowly enough for proper annealing.

If you have a fiber-insulated kiln, you must regulate the temperature drop. Slow the rate of cooling so that it takes about an hour to drop from annealing or around 970°F (521°C) to 850°F (454°C). This is the *strain temperature point*—the lowest temperature at which glass can release stress, i.e., stress that develops below that temperature through the cooling process is only temporary. Hold the kiln at this temperature for 15 minutes before turning it off. The balance of the annealing process happens as the kiln slowly drops to room temperature. Don't open the kiln while it's still hot, since this can lead to thermal shock.

To control the drop in temperature on a kiln with only an infinite switch, you must do this manually by lowering the number (on the switch) at which the kiln is set and watch the kiln. A kiln wired to a computerized temperature controller can be programmed ahead of time to complete the cycle for you. There are controllers available that are pre-programmed for soft glass (COE 104) or can be pre-programmed as needed for other formulas.

If you're using a brick-lined kiln and are not getting good results from simply shutting the kiln off (i.e., beads are still cracking after the annealing cycle), take the time to watch the drop in temperature, and see how long it takes to cool to the strain point. If this happens in less than an hour, then you'll need to control the temperature drop as described above for a fiber-insulated kiln.

Annealing Cooled Beads

As we've already said, the best way to assure successful cooling is to put a hot bead directly from flame annealing at the torch into a kiln pre-heated to annealing temperature. Since this is not always practical, you can allow the beads to first cool in a thermal blanket or vermiculite. After removing them from the mandrels and cleaning them, put the beads into a room-temperature kiln, heat it up slowly to annealing temperature (this should take no less than 30 minutes), soak the beads, and cool them as previously outlined.

Removing Beads from the Mandrel

After the beads have cooled to room temperature on their mandrels, soak them in a bowl full of room-temperature water. This will soften the release a bit and keep the dust from it out of the air.

With one hand, grip the mandrel close to the bead with a pair of pliers, and loosen the bead with your other hand (photo 1). If the bead doesn't slide off easily, use pliers to hold the mandrel and a piece of flat, flexible rubber to grip the bead so that you can loosen it (photo 2).

If the beads are stubborn and won't come loose, soak them longer, or overnight, to soften the release a bit more. If this doesn't do it, you can

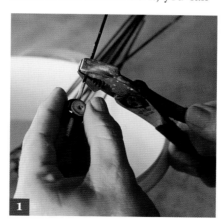

secure the mandrel in a vice to get a really tight grip on the bead while you try to pull it off. Try not to bend the mandrel while loosening the bead.

Some beadmakers find it useful to use a motorized grinding wheel to loosen beads. First, crumble the dampened bead release from the mandrel's tip. Turn on the grinding wheel, and then hold the mandrel's tip against it. The vibration of it on the wheel will loosen the bead so that it slides off easily.

As the final step to making a bead, use a bead hole reamer to scrape out any residual release from inside the bead. Remove as much as possible, and then rinse it out with water. Repeat this several times (photo 3). The hole will retain a rough, etched look, even after you've cleaned it.

Once you've practiced making basic beads and are comfortable with the process and successful, you can pick and choose from the exciting techniques that follow in the next chapter.

After you've mastered making basic beads, you'll be in the enviable position of taking the next steps while you develop more skills and expand your repertoire. This chapter covers simple shaping techniques and the addition of color to the base bead. As you work through these techniques, you fine-tune your beadmaking skills, particularly your ability to read heat and continue to work with gravity.

Shaping Beads

In the section that follows, you'll explore ways to shape various kinds of beads. For instance, you can use the flat surface of a marver or paddle to roll or press the bead, lending it a more defined shape. In addition, you can use patterned marvers to shape the surface of a molten bead.

When you shape beads on a marver, position the marver close to the edge of your work surface on the side of the torch where you hold the mandrel so you won't have to reach across the torch. Hold the mandrel in your hand away from the table's edge and parallel to the marver as you roll the bead (photo 1).

Barrel Beads

A barrel bead is the easiest shaped bead to make. To make this kind of bead, begin by heating a symmetrical bead (either round or long) to a bright orange glow (photo 2) before bringing it out of the flame. Continue to turn the bead and keep it symmetrical. Allow the glow of the bead to fade from bright orange to dull orange. At this point, roll the bead on the marver to straighten the sides, keeping the mandrel parallel.

Roll the bead back and forth a few times, applying slight pressure while the glass is still soft. Don't press too hard at this point, or you might push the whole bead off center or break it loose from the mandrel. Increase the pressure slightly as the bead cools and firms up. If needed, reheat and roll the bead on the marver a few times to get to the shape you want.

You can also use a graphite paddle to shape this kind of bead, as well as other shaped beads. The graphite is lightweight and doesn't draw a lot of heat from the bead. Balancing the paddle on top of the torch, roll the bead as you would on a marver. You'll be able to look at the bead more closely while you work (photo 3).

An overhand paddling technique works well if you want to get a good perspective of exactly how you're shaping the bead. To do this, hold the paddle above the bead. The mandrel should be parallel to the paddle. Push the bead up onto the paddle while rolling it. This technique also allows you to keep the bead closer to the flame so that you can reheat it easily. It might take a while to get the hang of it, but it is very efficient (photo 4).

A paddle also works well for evening up the ends of the bead. After the bead heats to a dull orange glow, take it out of the flame. Hold the paddle at the end of the bead at a right angle to the mandrel, resting lightly on it (photo 5). Roll the bead allowing the paddle to even up the end. Don't press the glass in past the point that it has already made contact with the mandrel. Also, avoid pressing the paddle so hard that you cut into the bead release. Reheat the bead and repeat this movement if the glass doesn't even up the first time.

2

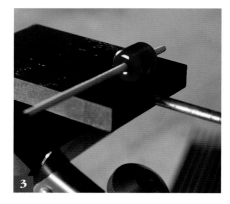

3

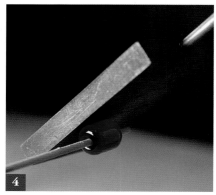

4

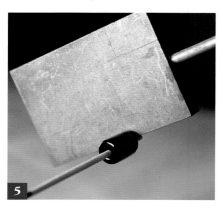

5

> **NOTE**
>
> *Be sure to roll the bead along the marver rather than dragging it. In the future, when you add a design to a bead, you'll distort it if you drag the glass. So get in the habit of doing this correctly now.*

Rounded/ Oblong Beads

To form a rounded or oblong bead, wrap the molten glass up and down the mandrel to build it up. Heat the bead to a dull orange glow, and use gravity to make the bead symmetrical. Roll the bead back and forth on a hand-held graphite paddle, changing the angle at which you roll the bead to shape it (photos 6 and 7).

(In the example shown, notice that the bead has also been moved to the edge of the paddle to accommodate the angle of the mandrel. This positioning also helps to shape the ends of the bead.)

6

7

Cones

In this section, you'll learn to create a cone-shaped bead. First wind a round bead that is heavier on one end but evenly shaped around the mandrel (photo 8). Now heat this bead until it is a dull orange.

Hold the graphite paddle in your dominant hand. Hold the mandrel at an angle to the paddle with the thin end of the bead about ¼ inch (6 mm) from the edge of it. Roll

8

9

the bead to smooth the sides of the cone so that they're straight (photo 9). Placing the bead close to the edge of the paddle allows the glass to move toward the narrow end of the bead and create a small indentation. Remember that the end shouldn't be too pointed, or it might chip.

To flatten the wide end/bottom of it, reheat the bead to a dull orange glow and place the paddle against it at a right angle to the mandrel. Roll the bead to smooth and flatten the bottom (photo 10). Reheat it, and repeat this move as needed to make it flat.

During the process of making this bead, you might need to switch back and forth between rolling the angled side and flattening the bottom as you work toward the shape that you want. Reheat the bead to a dull orange glow between each paddling.

10

Bicones

Next, you'll learn to make a bicone bead. This bead looks like two cones with their wide bases joined together. Begin by winding a long bead that is slightly shorter than the desired length and is thicker in the middle. Be sure the bead is evenly shaped around the mandrel (photo 11).

Heat half of the bead to a dull orange glow, and roll it at an angle as you did the cone, forming a narrow end. Be sure to allow a little bit of glass to move toward the end of the bead to create the desired indentation (photo 12).

Heat the opposite end of the bead, and tip the mandrel in the other direction before rolling the other end (photo 13). Note in the photo that the overhand marvering method can be used for this shaping also (photo 14).

You may have to reheat and roll each end a few times in order to create a symmetrical bead. You can center the widest part of the bead, where the two cones meet, or you can choose to make the bead asymmetrical. In other words, you can create interesting variations of this design by shortening one cone in relation to a longer one.

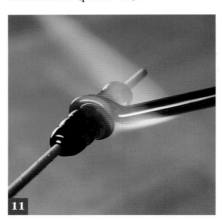

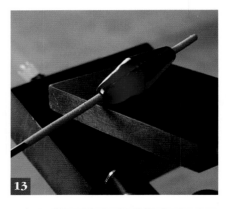

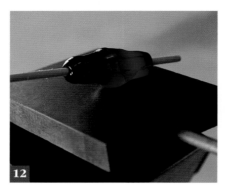

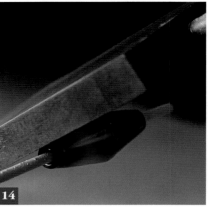

Pressed Beads

You can flatten two or more sides of a bead on a marver or with a parallel press to create beads of various shapes. Flattening two sides forms a disc or tabular-shaped bead, three sides forms a triangular-shaped bead, and four sides makes a cube.

To make the simplest version, heat a bead to a bright orange glow, and press it down lightly, parallel to the marver (photo 15). Flip the bead over, and press it to flatten the other side. You may need to reheat the bead and repeat this process to get the desired shape.

However, don't overdo it, since the thickness of the area along the mandrel should be at least as great as the mandrel's diameter. The bead won't cool properly if the glass is too thin, and it is likely to crack and/or break. (Photo 16 shows that the top side of the bead has been flattened too much because the area along the mandrel is thinner than the mandrel itself.)

15

16

If you wish to create a triangular, square, or multi-faceted bead, flatten the sides lightly the first time around so that you can check the shape before refining it further. Then reheat the bead before pressing it again. You can use a graphite paddle to even up the ends, if needed.

You can also use a parallel press to make pressed beads. Heat the bead until it is very molten, and sandwich it between the paddles before squeezing them together. Flatten it a bit, take a look at it, and then reheat and flatten it more if you wish. This tool guarantees perfect parallel sides (photo 17).

17

18

49

Disc Beads

To create a narrow, disc-shaped bead, you'll wind glass on top of glass to build the shape outwards from the mandrel. If you plan to eventually decorate the narrow disc shape (such as adding dots to it), consider using a bead release that has more "grip" to it. This will allow you to decorate the bead with less concern about loosening it while you work.

Begin making this bead by touching the glass down lightly on the mandrel, with a small amount of contact, to keep the width of the bead very narrow. Wind the molten glass around the mandrel as you rotate it away from you. Keep the bead narrow and don't drift off center, keeping the first wrap very

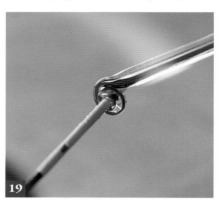

straight to prevent a rough edge around the bead's hole (photo 19).

Drop the mandrel and bead beneath the flame, so that it cools slightly and begins to stiffen. Push the rod through the flame to reach the bead. Continue to slowly rotate the mandrel away from you as the new glass heats to molten. Pull more glass onto the rotating bead, winding it on so that the disc shape begins to form.

Continue to wrap the glass by rotating the mandrel. As you build up more glass on the bead, you'll need to move it down gradually from the flame so that the

NOTE

In the photos that show winding a disc bead, we've used filigrana *glass rod so that the trail of the glass is more obvious.*

wrapped glass has a chance to cool and firm up slightly, allowing the new glass to build up effectively (photo 20). Wind the glass until the height of your bead is slightly more than you wish for the final bead, and flame-cut the rod from the bead.

Continue to heat the bead with the mandrel slightly below the flame. Allow the glass to soften and relax a bit to create indentations around the mandrel. Use a graphite paddle to smooth the sides of the bead and keep it tall, if needed. When you do this, use very light pressure, since the bead is very narrow in width (photo 21).

After you've shaped your disc, you can decorate it or leave it plain. If you do decorate it, you'll find it easier to hold the mandrel at a different angle. (Here, we're placing dots on the side of the bead, holding the mandrel at an angle [photo 22]). Hold the bead out of the flame as much as possible while you decorate it, reheating it in the cooler part of the flame as needed. This will keep the disc from slumping out of shape.

19

21

20

22

"Groovy" Patterned Beads

Patterned marvers allow you to alter a bead's surface, creating some wonderful effects. The angle at which you hold the marver will alter the design, and you can roll a bead vertically, horizontally, or diagonally in relation to the marver's design.

Start by trying out a grooved marver to make a bead with ridges. Position the marver on the side of the torch next to your dominant hand, near the edge of the work surface. Then form a barrel-shaped bead (see page 46). Heat the bead until it glows medium orange before you begin to roll it.

To indent grooves straight around the circumference, lightly roll the hot bead on the grooves in one direction, all the way around, until the grooves meet. Then roll the bead back in the other direction to deepen the grooves (photo 23). As the glass cools and firms, increase the pressure on it while you roll it.

To press angled grooves into the bead, change the position of the marver in relationship to the mandrel. With the marver angled, still flat on the table, use medium pressure to roll the bead around only once until the grooves on the bead meet (photo 24). The grooves on this type of bead are difficult to align if you go back over them.

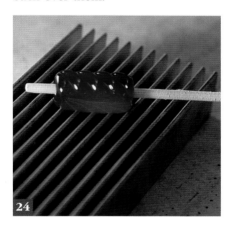

To create a crosshatching or a "pineapple" effect, reheat a bead that has been grooved at an angle until it glows a dull orange, then roll it again at an angle approximately 90° to your first set of lines.

Rolling the bead on a patterned marver will chill the bead considerably, so you must reheat it to a dull red to even out its temperature, and prevent it from cracking as it cools. Turn the bead in the tip of the flame until the glow returns, but don't allow it to get too molten, or your design will melt away.

Alternative Patterned Surfaces

You can create patterned beads with found objects such as files, rasps, or even serving spoons with decorative patterns. Look around at flea markets and junk sales for patterned surfaces that are metal, clay, or another material that can withstand the heat of glass. Keep in mind that the patterns must be small enough to fit the bead and be visually effective. Clean each surface thoroughly so that the bead doesn't pick up debris from it.

You can also carve your own pattern into graphite or clay to make a unique surface for lending texture to a bead.

If you're using hand tools, use sharp tools such as those made for carving wood, jewelry wax for casts, or linoleum blocks for printmaking. Since graphite powder is dangerous to inhale, hold it under water while carving it or dampen it beforehand. This will be a messy job, but the resulting surfaces will be unique.

Handheld drills have a wide variety of bits that make excellent carving tools, and a motorized tool will expedite the carving process. Dampen the surface of the graphite before you carve it, and rinse it continuously to remove the excess graphite.

Flattened pieces of clay can be impressed with other patterned objects or carved before they are fired. Obviously, the items that you use to make impressions don't have to be heat-resistant (you can impress with plastic or even cloth, for instance). After you finish the surface, you'll need to air-dry it and bisque-fire it (one firing) in the kiln. You can use your beadmaking kiln for this, but you'll need to get some help from a ceramist to guide you in the firing. How this firing is done will depend on the kind of clay purchased.

After firing, soak the bisque-fired clay mold in water so that it is damp when it is used to impart shape to a molten bead. Steam is released when the hot bead is pressed into the damp mold, and this dampness keeps the bead from sticking to the mold.

Found objects, such as a patterned spoon can be used as marvers. You can also carve graphite or clay to make a patterned marver.

Adding Color & Decoration

After you've experimented with shaping single-colored beads, you can stack various colors or embellish the surface of beads with exciting patterns. The following section covers some of the many ways of combining colors in a single bead to create an infinite number of designs.

Stacking Colors

One very simple way to create a multi-colored bead is wrapping two or more colors next to each other on the mandrel. To create a bead with two colors, begin by wrapping a basic bead. Allow the bead to cool a bit while continuing to turn it and keep it on center. After the glow is gone, keep warming it in the back flame (moving it in and out quickly) to prevent cracking. Then heat a second color, and wrap another basic bead right next to the first so that they touch (photo 1). (Each color you add should have its own mound or bulge of glass as shown.)

Next, heat the whole bead until it rounds off and smoothes out. Lightly roll it on a marver to move a small amount of glass out to the ends to create indentations (photo 2).

To add a third or fourth color to your design, wrap each of the individual colors, and allow each wrap to cool and firm up before adding the next one. As each additional color is wrapped, try to keep the previously wrapped colors away from the direct heat of the flame so that they remain cool enough to keep their shape. This will keep each band of color more distinct when you heat and shape the final bead.

To keep air bubbles from getting trapped when you're stacking a color next to another one, make sure that the color you add is very molten. Nudge the molten glass against the side of the previously wrapped color.

Once you've wrapped the colors of your choice, heat the whole bead and marver it to smooth it out. Make sure the ends are well formed and indented.

Surface Decoration

The surface of a bead lends you a great opportunity to work with more color and decoration. This section introduces you to some of the main ways of doing this, including using *frit* (ground glass), *dots, stringers* (thin strands of glass), or *twists* (combined glass strands). These applications are a springboard for an unlimited number of variations.

Applying Frit

Frit, or ground bits of glass in various sizes and colors, can be added to the hot surface of a bead to create a random spotted pattern. This is the simplest way to decorate a bead with color. Frit can be purchased in sample packets from most glass beadmaking suppliers so that you can experiment with color combinations. You can also make your own frit (see page 55).

To add frit to a bead, sprinkle it on a smooth heatproof surface such as a marver. Heat the bead until it is a bright orange, and roll it in the frit (photo 1). The hot glass will pick up the crushed glass bits. Since the bead is very molten at this point, roll it with light pressure to keep it from being pushed off center.

Put the bead back in the flame to *fuse* the frit to it (photo 2). For a textured look, fuse the frit with just enough heat to allow it to settle into the surface and keep it attached to the bead. For a smooth surface, melt the frit completely with additional heat and light marvering. If you want to add more frit to the surface, simply reheat the bead and roll it in the frit again.

You can also apply frit to a bead from a shallow spoon. Fill the spoon with frit and hold it beneath the flame. Lower the molten bead to the spoon, roll it in the frit, and then take the bead back to the flame (photo 3). This technique makes it easier to cover a rounded bead and helps keep different colors of frit cleanly separated. To achieve depth in the surface decoration, alternate layers of transparent and opaque frit.

MAKING YOUR OWN FRIT: You can make your own frit by one of two methods. For the first, heat the end of a glass rod to form a hot orange ball (photo 4). Then flatten it with a parallel press (photo 5) or with a paddle on top of a marver. Reheat the disc of glass until it glows again, and then plunge it into a small bowl of water so that it fractures into small pieces (photos 6 and 7).

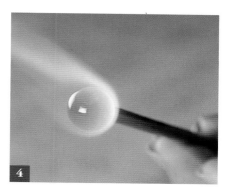

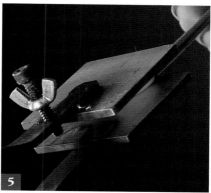

Repeat this process of making a disk and fracturing it until a small amount of frit accumulates in the dish. Strain the frit by pouring the contents of the bowl into a kitchen strainer lined with paper towels. Spread out the frit to dry, allowing the water to evaporate before using it.

This process will produce several sizes of frit that might need sorting. Melt the larger pieces again by placing them on a marver and picking them up with a molten ball of glass. Melt them into the ball of glass before repeating the above steps. The color of the frit might change slightly when you do this, especially light opaque colors. When you add frit to a bead, reheat it, and then cool it, the original color will return.

You can also make frit by using a glass crusher. To make a crusher, use two short sections of steel pipe with threaded caps that fit together snugly, with the smaller one inside the larger one. The crusher pictured on page 20 is made from two pieces of galvanized nipple (short lengths of plumbing pipe that have threads on both ends), one that is 6 inches (15.2 cm) long and 1½ inches (3.8 cm) in diameter, and the other that is 8 inches (20.3 cm)

long and ¾ inch (1.9 cm) in diameter. Each has an appropriately sized threaded cap. The cap for the smaller pipe fits into the larger one, so when you buy these pieces at a hardware or home improvement store, test the two to make sure that they fit together.

To smash the glass, use tile nippers to break off short pieces of glass that are about an inch (2.5 cm) long, and place them in the bottom of the larger pipe. Slip the capped end of the smaller pipe into the larger one. Hold onto both pieces of pipe, and slam the smaller one into the larger one, crushing the glass inside.

If you'd like to separate the frit into different sizes, use mesh screens or enamel sifters of various sizes to do this. When you use the steel pipe to grind up the glass, tiny bits of metal will be deposited into the frit. If these bits are picked up on a bead, they will be very visible and create an uneven surface. Sift these metal bits out of the larger-sized frit using a larger mesh screen. Use a magnet to pull this metal out of the smaller, sugar-sized frit.

You can also buy a crusher through a beadmaking supplier. Even though it costs more, this tool allows you to crush frit without adding bits of metal to it. This tool is especially worth having if you want to make a lot of frit in a color that's not readily available.

Making Dots

In contrast to the random patterns created by frit, you can add dots to the surface of your bead in a controlled manner. Making dots is simple and fun, and you can vary them or layer them to make different designs.

Begin by making a core bead of any shape. Allow it to cool slightly until the glow is gone from it. Keep the bead warm in the back of the flame. With your dominant

hand, heat a glass rod so that the tip is molten and rounds off (photo 1).

With the rod and bead out of the flame, touch the rod straight down onto the bead's surface, so that the rod is perpendicular to it (photo 2). Pull the rod away from the bead about $1/2$ inch (1.3 cm).

The glass rod will still be connected to the bead by a thread. Use the flame to cut the rod from the bead (photo 3). Be sure that the glass rod is completely separated before pulling it away from the bead so

that you don't create a thin hair of glass that's difficult to control. Aim the flame at the dot for a few seconds, and then bring the bead out of the flame. Turn the mandrel so that the dot is on top of the bead. It will round off and sink into the bead's surface (photo 4, next page). This is only the initial placement of the dot.

After the initial placement of your dots, leave them raised or melt them so that they're flush with the bead's surface. If you create dots of a consistent size, it will be easier to round them all off evenly in the flame.

NOTE

The amount of glass left behind on the bead is determined by how much pressure you use on the rod. If you barely touch the bead's surface, only a bit of glass will stick. More pressure will result in more glass on the bead's surface. It's best to lay down too little glass the first time and then add to it if needed. Otherwise, you'll find yourself trying to remove the excess glass with tweezers.

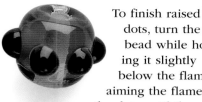

To finish raised dots, turn the bead while holding it slightly below the flame, aiming the flame at the dots until they melt to a point that is just short of what you want (photo 5). Take the bead out of the flame to check the dots while you're working, since they melt and settle quickly. Keep in mind that since they'll still be hot when you bring them out of the flame, the dots will settle a bit more before they cool. If one dot seems to need more heat than the others, single it out and hold it directly beneath the flame before lifting it back up.

To completely melt the dots, position the bead slightly below the flame, and heat the bead's surface until the dots are flush with it. Try to keep the center of the bead cool and firm, since heating the entire bead will make the glass more difficult to control. (If the center is cooler, the glass will appear darker close to the mandrel.) You can also use a graphite paddle to push the dots into the surface while you work, holding the paddle beneath or above the bead (photos 6 and 7).

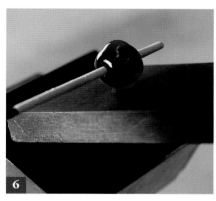

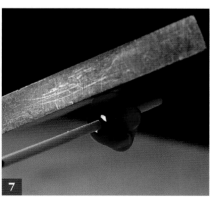

Positioning Dots Precisely

If you want to position dots evenly around a bead, place a first dot, and then put a dot on the mandrel in line with this one (photo 8). Turn the bead all the way around and place a dot on the bead directly opposite the first one, using the mandrel dot as a guide (photo 9).

Now that you have two reference points on the bead, fill in dots evenly between the two dots. With practice, it will become easier to do this. Careful placement of the dots can truly enhance the design.

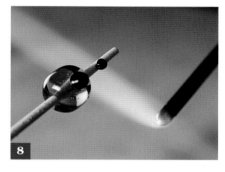

Dot Variations

After you practice making dots and learn to place equal-sized ones exactly where you want them, you can use those simple dots in many creative ways. The following section introduces you to some of the variations of this technique that you can use to enhance your beads.

STACKED DOTS: You can add even more dimension, patterning, and color to a bead by stacking smaller dots on top of your core ones. If you want them to remain raised, be sure to heat stacked dots enough to fuse them well to the dot underneath. If you plan on making a very tall stack of dots (more than four layers), it helps to flatten the top of each dot slightly with a palette knife before adding the next dot.

To make both dots (or subsequent dots) flush with the bead's surface to create a circular pattern, add the second layer of dots before melting the first one completely into the surface. The raised surface will provide you with an easier target for your glass rod (photo 1).

TILE EFFECT: To create an interesting and beautiful surface on your bead, you can make a tile effect using dots. To do this, position dots close to one another, without touching, so that a bit of the underlying color on the bead shows. As the dots melt, they spread out on the bead's surface, bumping into each other and altering one another. The shapes remain separated by a thin line of the underlying color.

OVERLAID DOTS: Dots can also be laid over previously placed rows to create a design that resembles the scales of a fish. To create this effect, lay down a row of dots evenly around a bead, placing them relatively close together without allowing them to touch (photo 2). Dot a second color of glass over this first row, and heat the bead's surface until the dots are flush with it. (Using a transparent glass as the second color will create a more three-dimensional look.)

To continue making the pattern on the bead, lay down a second row of dots slightly over and between each dot in the first row. Repeat the process of stacking the dots by adding the second color on this row. Allow these stacked dots to melt into the surface (photo 3). Continue overlapping rows of dots as desired.

MASKED DOTS: You can vary overlaid dots slightly by using opaque colors and offsetting the second dot color. To use this technique, lay down the first dot on your base bead and let it melt in completely. Use the same color as the base bead to create the second dot, placed over from the center of the first one so that it contacts part of it and part of the base bead, leaving a crescent shape visible (thus the "masking"). This concept has many variations such as laying two or more small dots on or around the edge of a large one or using more than two colors. Experimentation is the key to developing beautiful patterns.

BUBBLE DOTS: This technique is used to purposefully trap air bubbles near the surface of the glass where you've laid down dots, lending your bead a three-dimensional look. Begin by laying down a pattern of dots on the bead in an opaque color. Melt these dots almost all the way in before laying down clear or transparent colored dots on top of them, almost

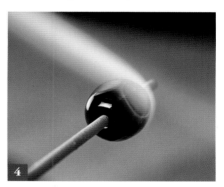

completely covering them. Then melt the layered glass flush into the bead's surface. Let the bead cool until the glow is almost gone, so the bead firms up a bit prior to the next step.

Heat one dot until it has a dull orange glow (photo 4). Plunge your tungsten pick straight down into the center of it, leaving an indentation behind (photo 5). Repeat this process, and work around the bead to indent all the dots.

Cap each plunged dot with a dot of transparent molten glass, trapping air in the indentation (photo 6). Heat the dots until they've melted in completely, creating bubbles in the center of each dot.

> **NOTE**
>
> *As you rake, don't push the end of the tool into the bead—keep it on the surface. A small amount of glass will stick to the rake. It will probably be molten enough to flame-cut it easily from the bead. After this, put the rake in your quenching bowl to shock the glass so that it pops off. If this doesn't work the first time, reheat the tip of the rake again, and chill it again. Remove this glass so that you don't unintentionally add it to a bead later on.*

RAKED DOTS: The shape of round dots can be altered in several ways. The simplest way is by raking them. To do this, lay down a series of dots around a bead, and stack a few colored dots on each of them. Melt the dots in all the way and reshape the bead, if needed. Allow the bead to cool until the glow is gone from it so that the inner part is firm.

Hold the bead in your non-dominant hand and the bead rake in your other hand. Hold the bead at the top of the flame with the flame hitting the bottom of it. (During this process, you should only heat the surface of the bead, not the whole bead, or you might distort it.) Position the rake so that the point will come in contact with the bead's surface as you slowly rotate the bead and the section you just heated comes up out of the flame (photo 7). This section will now be visible so that you can see what you're doing as you rake it. Continue to turn the bead and rake through the dots all the way around it.

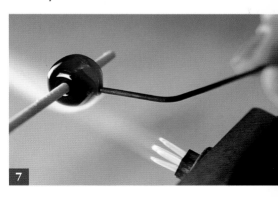

DOTS WITH CLEAR WRAPS: If you add a wrap of clear glass on top of dots and melt it in, the clear glass will spread out, moving and stretching the dots so that an interesting pattern develops on the bead's surface. A couple of ways to do this are described below.

For one option, place dots diagonally across from one another on a round bead, and stack them with dots of transparent color (photo 8). Begin to melt the dots into the surface (photo 9). Melt them in so that they're flush with the surface, and then add a clear wrap twice around the bead's equator (photo 10). This motion is like wrapping a disc

bead. With the bead beneath the flame, rotate it so that the flame hits only the wrap and melts it in evenly (photo 11). As the wrap sinks into the bead's surface, the dots are pulled toward each other, making a triangular pattern (photo 12).

As another option, add a clear wrap over raised dots (photo 13). Hold this tall bead below the flame (as you did in the previous technique), rotating it so that the flame hits the wrap and dots. Use a graphite paddle to straighten the wrap so that it melts in evenly, pulling or spreading the dots into stripes on the bead (photo 14).

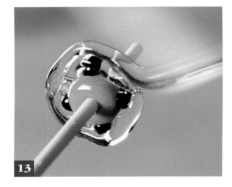

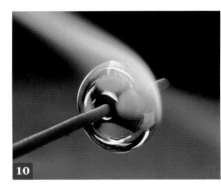

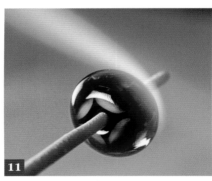

Making and Using Stringers

A stringer is a thin strand of glass that can be used to decorate beads in various ways. You can buy stringers in one standard thickness and a variety of colors, or make your own. The following section introduces you to how to make stringers and variations and then wrap them on beads, draw with them, and use them as tools.

To make a simple stringer, begin by heating the end of a glass rod to form a pea-sized ball of molten glass. Bring the glass out of the flame and pinch a very small amount with a pair of tweezers or bent-nosed pliers (photo 1).

Allow the bright orange glow to fade to a dull orange, and then pull the glass into a thin strand (this will only take a few seconds). As you do this, the glass will begin to cool and become rigid, making it more difficult to pull. Give it a last little tug at this point, and hold the stringer taut for a second or two to keep it straight as it cools (photo 2). (A straight stringer is much easier to use than a curved one.) Flame-cut the stringer from the rod, so that it separates completely.

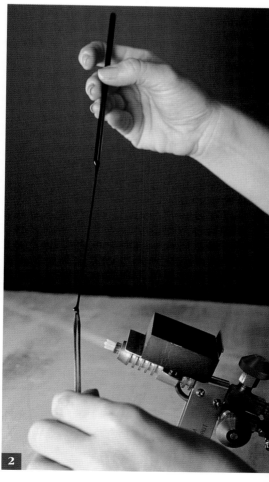

Try to make stringers that are about 12 to 14 inches (30.5 to 35.6 cm) with a thickness similar to thin spaghetti. The stringer's thickness is determined by how molten the glass is and how quickly you pull it. As you learn to work with stringers, you'll learn to use different thicknesses for various effects.

If you're working on a bead and find that you don't have a stringer in a color you need, you can quickly make one without compromising your work. Keep the bead warm while you do this. Heat a smaller amount of glass rod than you would for a regular stringer. Touch the molten glass lightly onto a preheated, release-coated spot on the mandrel, and begin pulling it into a stringer (photo 3). Pause a few seconds with the stringer still connected to the mandrel as the glass firms up. Pull the stringer from the mandrel (photo 4).

You'll break off some bead release when you do this. To remove it, heat the end of the stringer to molten. Chill it in your quenching bowl so that the end pops off, taking the bead release with it. Now your stringer is ready to use.

STRIPED STRINGERS: It's fairly easy to make striped stringers that can be applied to beads to add more color and create a different pattern. To do this, heat a glass rod, and form a small ball of molten glass at the end of it. Flatten it into a disc by mashing it between a marver and graphite paddle or use a parallel press. Heat a second color to molten, and use the rod to paint a stripe down the center of the disc (photo 5). Separate the rod by flame-cutting it. Heat the disc to molten, and bring it out of the flame.

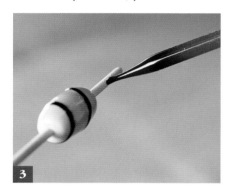

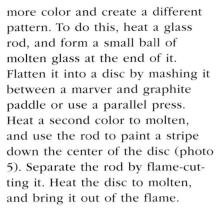

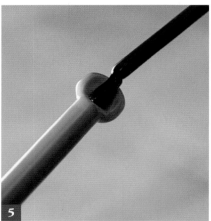

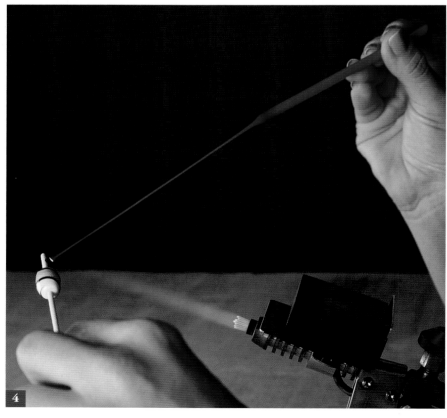

Use tweezers to pinch a bit of both colors of glass, and wait two to three seconds before you pull the glass out into a stringer (photo 6, previous page). (Later, when you apply this type of stringer to a bead, you'll keep the stripe on top as it is applied to the bead.)

To make a stringer with more stripes, paint another color down the other side of the disc and pull the stringer as usual. When you apply this type of stringer, flip it to show both stripes.

ENCASED STRINGERS: You can create a wonderful visual effect by *encasing* ("casing") the end of a glass rod with another rod before pulling it into a stringer. Most commonly, you'll case an opaque colored glass rod with clear or transparent colored glass so that a thin line of the core color can be seen inside the stringer. The support of the clear or transparent glass is important, since a very thin stringer of color that isn't encased is difficult to apply.

In addition, there are some glass colors that tend to spread out when

added to the bead's surface, such as light opaque colors, especially greens, and encasing these colors keeps this from happening. When an encased stringer is applied, the color in the stringer will be lifted slightly from the bead's surface due to the transparent layer.

You can also experiment with other color combinations. For instance, very dark transparent purple (which is seen as black) cased on a white or another light opaque color will make a beautiful stringer.

To case a rod, begin by holding the core rod in your non-dominant hand, and warm it in the end of the flame. Don't allow it to get hot enough to slump with heat. Hold the clear or transparent glass (your casing color) in your dominant

hand, and bring a small ball of glass to molten. With the rods out of the flame, push the molten casing color about 1 inch (2.5 cm) down the side of the core rod (photo 7). Pull the casing color away from the core rod, and cut it in the flame.

Heat another small ball of the casing color to molten, and push it down the core rod next to your first stripe. Work around the core rod until it's completely encased (photo 8). Use a bit more molten glass to cap the end of the rod (photo 9).

Heat the cased section of the rod until it begins to soften with heat, and then roll it on a marver or paddle to smooth it (photo 10). To be sure that the rod is completely cased, heat the glass in the flame and check it to see if there is an area that glows more brightly. If a spot has been left uncovered, heat up the casing rod, and cover that area with a bit more molten encasing glass.

After all of this is done, take the rod out of the flame. Let it cool until it stops glowing. Reheat a portion of the encased section to molten, and pull your first stringer from it. You might get several pulls from the encased section.

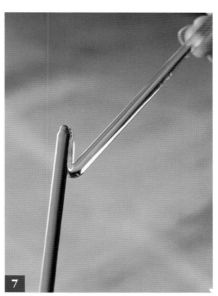
7

8

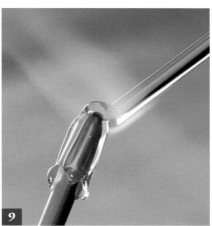
9

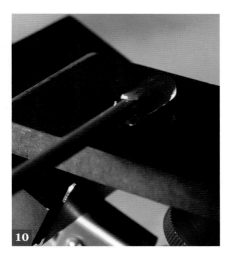
10

Wrapping Stringers

Wrapping a stringer on a bead for a decorative effect can be a bit tricky at first. However, it's really just a matter of finding the right spot in the flame so that you can control the process. When you're learning to wrap a stringer, start by wrapping a fairly thick one on a barrel or tubular-shaped bead, since it will be easier.

After shaping a bead, allow it to cool until the glow goes out of it and it firms up. Hold the stringer in your dominant hand, and place it underneath the flame, pointed up toward it at an angle. Hold the bead in your non-dominant hand.

When you first try doing this, hold the stringer and mandrel so that they form about a 45° angle with the vertex placed at the edge of the flame underneath it (photo 1).

Heat the end of the stringer to form a small molten ball at the end of it. Quickly lay down the end of the molten stringer at the top of the bead (photo 2). Lift the bead and stringer up to the lower edge of the flame so that the stringer heats and starts softening.

NOTE

The angle of the stringer in relation to the bead will determine how many times the wrap reaches around the bead. If the stringer is applied at an angle close to 90°, you can wrap it around and down the bead quite a few times. If you use a tighter angle, the stringer might only wrap around the bead once. Experiment with applying stringers to fully understand this concept.

Rotate the bead away from you as you pull the softened stringer onto it and wrap it around the bead (photo 3). Continue to heat the stringer in the bottom of the flame while you wrap it (sandwiching the stringer between the flame and bead). Stop wrapping the stringer at a point of your choice, and flame-cut it to remove it. Be sure that the stringer is completely separated from the bead before bringing it away from the flame.

If you plan to add more stringer wraps, keep the bead warmed at the end of the flame. If you let the bead cool off too much, the wraps you've already put on it can pop off when new ones are added.

When all the wraps have been added, you need to fuse them well. Heat them in the region of the flame that is cooler and adjacent to the hottest portion. Position the bead slightly beneath it, and heat the bead's surface all the way around so that you're fusing the wraps, without heating the whole bead. If you fuse the stringers well, they won't pop off when the bead cools.

To determine if the stringers are fused well, bring the bead out of the flame and hold it at eye level. Look closely at the bead to see that the cross section of the wrap forms a half-circle or dome on the bead's surface. There shouldn't be an undercut in any area where the stringer makes contact with the bead's surface. If you discover such an area, you'll need to go back to the flame and heat the wrap again to fuse it more, leaving the wrap as a ridge on the bead's surface.

Another option is to melt the wraps into the surface of the bead so that they're flush with it. To do this, continue the process of heating the surface until the wrap melts into it. Use a marver or paddle to smooth the bead as needed.

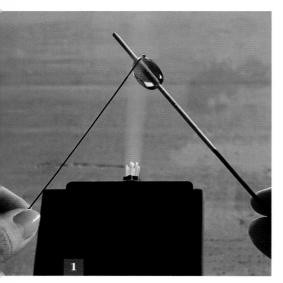

1

2

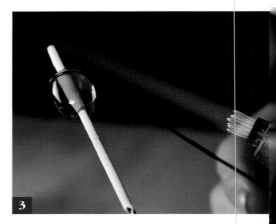

3

FEATHERING WRAPPED STRINGERS: You can create a different effect by feathering the wraps you've added. Begin by melting the wraps all the way into the bead's surface. Cool the bead until the glow goes out of it. Hold it in your non-dominant hand with a bead rake in your other hand. Position the bead slightly above and at a right angle to the flame. Lower the bead into the flame to heat a small section of it. Move the bead to the left and right to heat the whole length of it, if needed.

Bring the bead out of the flame, and position the rake at one end of the heated area (photo 4) before lightly pulling it through the wraps. Keep the rake on the surface of the bead so that you don't distort it.

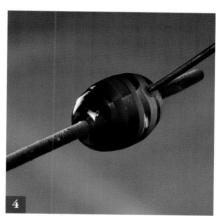

4

NOTE

If the rake sticks in the glass, take both out of the flame and allow them to cool off a bit. Wiggle the rake every couple of seconds until it loosens up. The rake will cool off more quickly than the glass. Cool the rake in the quenching bowl before raking through another heated section of the bead.

Rotate the bead to the next section you want to rake, and heat it up. Bring the bead out of the flame, and push through the wraps with the rake in the opposite direction (photo 5). Work your way around the bead, heating up a small section at a time, and pushing or pulling through the wraps to feather them.

The bead may need reshaping, depending on your preferences, once the feathering is done. Do this by heating it to a dull orange glow and paddling or marvering the bead into the shape of your choice. You might also choose to leave texture created by the strokes on the bead's surface.

5

Instead of a rake, you can use a serrated knife to feather wraps and create a different effect, since the knife will move all of the wraps at once.

Heat a section of the bead, and use the knife to pull the wraps about $1/8$ inch (3 mm). Heat the next section and stroke in the opposite direction (photo 6). Space the intervals between feathering as you wish, and reshape the bead as needed.

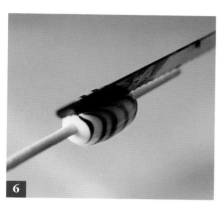

6

Drawing or Writing with Stringers

Drawing or writing with a stringer on a bead takes some practice but gives you lots of creative possibilities. In the beginning, use a stringer that is thick enough to work with easily. After this step, you can try a thinner one to create a more delicate effect.

Make a bead and let it cool until it's no longer glowing. Hold the stringer like a pencil in your dominant hand next to the flame with the bead in your non-dominant hand, just beneath the flame on the same side as the stringer. Turn the bead quickly in the flame to warm up the surface. Heat the stringer at the edge of the flame so that it softens slightly and can be moved around to draw various designs on the bead's surface (photos 1 and 2). Don't overheat the stringer, since it will get too molten and become difficult to control. With a bit of practice, you'll be able to draw or write with the stringer.

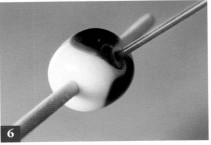

Making Dots with Stringers

You can also use stringers to make dots. Because they're thin, they're sometimes easier to use than a rod, such as trying to reach a tight spot to add dots between ridged wraps of glass or adding them at the end of a bead near the mandrel.

To do this, heat the end of the stringer at the edge of the flame to form a tiny ball on it (keeping in mind, of course, that stringers melt much more quickly than rods). Immediately touch this heated area down on the bead, and lift it slightly before flame-cutting it from the bead (photos 3 and 4).

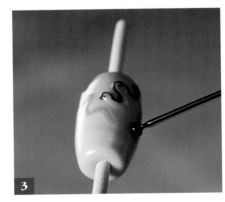

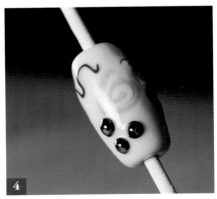

Using Stringers as Tools

Thicker stringers (up to ⅛ inch [3 mm] thick) can be used in the same way that some metal tools are used—to move glass on the surface of a bead, such as swirling or raking. At the same time, they add a bit of color to your bead.

TWIRLING DOTS WITH A STRINGER:

You can use a stringer as a tool to alter dots by twirling them. This twisting technique can also be used to alter the seam of two colors or to twirl parts of a stringer wrapped on a bead. Since a tiny bit of the stringer will remain behind, choose a color to match or complement the dots. Use a stringer about the thickness of regular spaghetti. Clip off the end of it with nippers or pliers before you start to make sure that you have a clean end.

Begin by laying down a series of dots close to each other but not touching, and melt them in flush

with the bead's surface. Let the bead cool until the glow has left the glass. Heat a spot between two dots to a bright orange glow (photo 5, previous page), and bring the bead out of the flame.

Push the clean end of the stringer into this space, pause a second, and then begin twisting it. Keep twisting until the glass either firms up or you get the effect you want (photo 6, previous page). Pause a moment, and then snap the stringer loose (photo 7). If it doesn't break loose at this point, wait a few seconds more or blow a little puff of air at the spot to chill it before you snap it again. Move to the adjacent spot between dots, heat the area, and twist again, continuing this process to finish the design (photo 8). As you work, you can twist in the same direction or alternate this movement to make a different pattern. The bead can be left as is or be reheated to molten and smoothed.

A wrapped and melted stringer can be twisted as well. Heat a small section of the wrap/stringer and twist and snap as just described. Move to a new spot, and then heat, twist, and snap again.

RAKING WITH A STRINGER: Instead of a bead rake, you can use a stringer to pull through wraps, squiggles, or dots. To create a small hook on the stringer, heat the end of it to molten, and use tweezers to pull a tiny bit of glass from it and to the side. Flame-cut the end in the flame. Let the tip of it cool a few seconds,

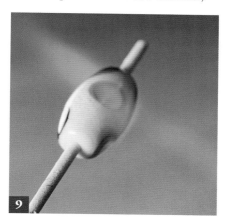

and then break off the excess portion of it by pushing it on the tabletop to create a sharp but fairly strong tip.

Make a bead and allow it to cool until it's no longer glowing. Spot-heat the area you want to alter until it is bright orange (photo 9). Bring the bead out of the flame, and drag the hooked stringer through the area. Pull the stringer away from the bead, taking a bit of the glass from the bead with it (photo 10). (This whole stroke should be done in one quick movement to prevent the stringer from leaving behind some of its color.) Flame-cut the tiny tail from the bead close to the surface. This technique leaves a sharper line than a metal rake.

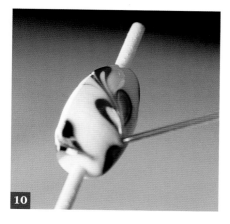

Twists

Twists are an advanced form of
a stringer that are used to decorate beads. You can combine
two or more colors to make
these interesting glass elements. They can be made with
an infinite number of color
combinations. Contrasting colors create a dramatic effect.
When you pull out transparent
colors, some will stay more visible than others. Dark transparent colors remain distinct while
pale ones almost disappear
when pulled out. Experiment
with various colors to find out
what works well. In this section, we'll explore several ways
to make twists and how to
apply them.

TWISTING TWO COLORS:
Choose two glass rod colors for
making your first twist. Use one
hand to warm the first color in the
flame's end, without heating it so
much that it softens, leaving it stiff.
Use your other hand to introduce
the second rod into the flame, and
heat about 1 inch (2.5 cm) of it to
molten, turning it to keep this area
centered and in shape as it softens
and becomes molten.

Overlap about 1 inch (2.5 cm) of
the second color on top of the first,
and place this overlapped area into
the flame (photo 1). Rotate it back
and forth to heat both sides. Don't
let your hands drift apart, or you'll
stretch the glass, making it difficult
to control as it becomes molten.
Try to keep from twisting the area
at this point, and keep the sections
of glass as straight and aligned
as possible.

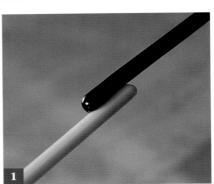

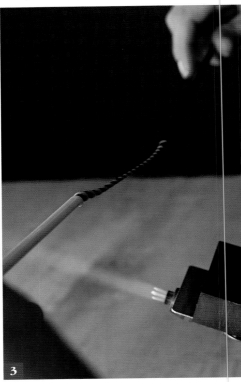

As you continue to heat it, the molten area will change and eventually take on a football-like shape. At first, there will be a darker line at the seam between the two colors that doesn't glow as brightly. Turn and heat the glass until this line glows as brightly as the rest of the shape (photo 2, previous page). This indicates that the glass is evenly heated.

Bring this area out of the flame, and pause for about three seconds, letting the bright orange glow fade slightly. Start twisting the rods in opposite directions with a motion resembling wringing water from a cloth. Pull your hands apart slightly, and twist it as quickly as possible (photo 3, previous page). As you continue to pull, keep the length of glass as horizontal as possible.

Continue to twist and pull until the glass cools and stiffens. As with a stringer, give the twist a last pull to straighten it; this will make it easier to apply later. An ideal length for a twist is about 12 inches (30.5 cm). Your first attempts will probably yield shorter twists until you learn to coordinate your hand and arm movements to optimize the timing prior to cooling.

After the twisted glass between the rods cools, flame-cut one end from a rod. Use wet, cool tweezers or pliers to chill the other end of the twist and break it off from the effect of thermal shock. (Photo 4 shows the broken end.) As another option, you can hold the twist with a pair of tweezers while you flame-cut the other end that's still attached.

TWISTING THREE COLORS: To make a twist with three colors, you'll elaborate on what you've learned. Any three colors can be used for this technique, but highly contrasting opaque colors work

well. The order of the colors (even if you're using the same three) will alter the look of the finished twist. The color that is sandwiched in the middle will affect the overall look of the twist.

To make a tri-colored twist, use your non-dominant hand to warm the first rod in the back of the flame without allowing the glass to soften or slump. The second color that you heat should be the one that you want to end up in the middle of the twist. While keeping the first rod warm in the back flame, heat about 3/4 inch (1.9 cm) of the second one to molten. Lay the molten glass onto the pre-warmed section of the first rod (photo 5). Separate the second rod in the flame, leaving the molten glass on the first rod.

Position the glass so that the flame hits *only* the second color with a glancing flame (photo 6). This means that you'll be holding the glass so that the flame hits it obliquely or at an angle, keeping intense heat away from the first rod so that it stays rigid. Heat the second color until it glows bright orange. Use a graphite paddle to flatten out the glass a bit (photo 7).

Hold this rod in the back flame in your non-dominant hand, and bring the third color rod into the flame. Heat it to molten, turning it to keep the molten area centered and in shape. Lay it over the second color so that all three colors are stacked on top of each other, with the second color sandwiched in between (photo 8).

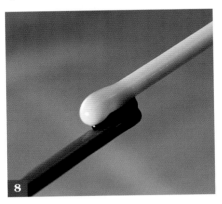

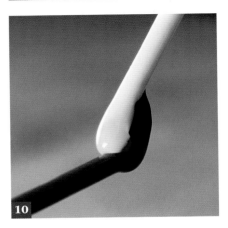

Connect the first and third colors at each end of the stacked glass by folding the top color down or the bottom color up so that it touches the other outer rod (photo 9). If the colors don't meet or aren't molten enough to fold, heat the area at one end of the overlaps, and tip the rods toward each other to bring the first and third colors together. Reverse this process, and bend the third color onto the first one on the other end of the stacked area (photo 10).

Now heat the whole overlapped area to molten as described above. You will have a bit more molten glass to control as you heat the overlapped area, so heat it slowly and don't let your hands drift apart. When this section is evenly heated, take it out of the flame and wait a few seconds. Pull, twist, and flame-cut the glass as described in the previous section on two-color twists. The finished twist will show a thin line of the sandwiched color between the other two colors. The twists shown in photo 11 were all created with the same colors, but each is different due to the placement of the middle color.

Applying Twists

Twists can be wrapped onto beads like a stringer, but they're easier to apply because they're usually thicker. To apply a twist, you'll sandwich it between the bottom of the flame

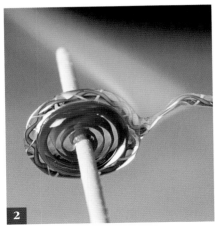

and the bead. Like a stringer, the twist should be warmed but not melted to apply it.

To apply a twist as a wrap, make one revolution around the bead. Use a twist that is about the thickness of spaghetti, heat the tip of it, and attach it. Then warm and soften it before wrapping it around the bead until it meets up at the starting point (photo 1, previous page).

At this point, bring the bead out of the flame and lift the twist, still connected to the bead, so that it is at a 90° angle to the bead's surface (photo 2, previous page). Put the bead back in the flame, and flame-cut the twist where the angle changes.

If the overlap of the glass is bumpy, heat *only* the excess glass to a bright orange glow. Touch the heated glass with the now-separated end of the twist, and pull away the extra molten glass (photo 3, previous page). Flame-cut the thin bit of glass that has been pulled away.

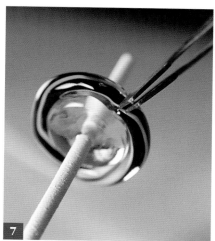

If you're using a thicker twist such as ribbon cane (see page 135), cut it with tile nippers rather than flame-cutting it. To do this, wrap the twist almost all the way around and take it out of the flame (photo 4). Estimate the length of twist that you need to complete the wrap, and nip the twist at this point (photo 5). Then warm the loose part of the twist, and guide it into place with tabular (flat-ended) tweezers (photo 6). Use the tweezers to pinch the glass slightly as the seam comes together (photo 7).

Use additional heat to fuse the twist onto the bead as desired. The twist must settle into the bead's surface as described with stringers. It can be left as a ridge or melted in completely (photo 8).

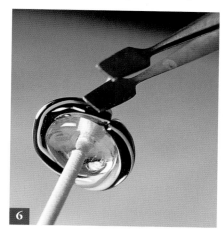

Trailing

Trailing is another method for decorating beads with a wrap. This method works best on a longer bead because you'll have more area to wrap.

Choose a colored rod for trailing to apply to your core bead. After making the bead, allow it to cool until the glow leaves it, and keep it warm in the back of the flame. Next, heat the end of the trailing rod until a small ball forms and glows bright orange. Move the bead and rod out of the flame, and touch the molten glass down lightly on the bead (photo 1).

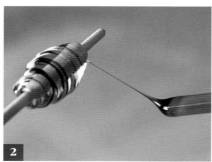

Pull the molten rod away from the bead so that a thin stringer forms. Quickly turn the bead away from you and pull the stringer onto it, continuing to pull the molten glass off the rod (photo 2). Continue wrapping trails until you get the effect that you want. (When you're first beginning to learn this technique, your wraps will probably be somewhat random [photo 3], but you can choose to make them more orderly as you learn to control the glass.) The faster you turn the bead, the thinner the wraps will be. Flame-cut the stringer from the bead when you've wrapped as much glass as you wish, or when you've pulled all of the molten glass from the rod.

You can leave trails as ridges, or melt them into the bead's surface. If ridged, be sure to melt them in enough to fuse them well to the bead (so that they won't break off later). You can add other trailing colors to your bead as you wish.

Applying Aventurine

In this section you'll learn how to apply aventurine to the surface of your bead to add a glittering sparkle to it. You can use aventurine frit or chunks of it to get different end results.

AVENTURINE FRIT: Aventurine frit behaves similarly to regular frit when you pick it up on a hot bead. However, it has to be protected from too much exposure to the flame by encasing it in clear or light transparent glass.

To apply aventurine frit, first pick up a layer of it on a hot bead (photo 1, below), and return the bead to the cooler part of the flame. Fuse the frit slightly (photo 2, next page). Avoid overheating it, or the frit will lose its metallic look.

Hold the bead in your non-dominant hand, and keep it warm in the back of the flame. Heat a clean rod of clear or light transparent glass until it's molten. Hold the rod up so that the glass slumps back on itself as it melts more. Continually rotate the rod of glass to keep the molten ball centered and under control.

Begin the encasing near one end of the bead, and avoid touching the

you reach the other end of the bead. Again, try not to touch the mandrel with the encasing glass (photo 4).

Continue adding glass until you've completely covered the aventurine frit, since even the smallest uncovered area will allow the frit to flow up onto the surface of the encasing glass. If this happens, it will glow brightly in the flame, so cover it with a small bit of very molten glass.

3

mandrel with the encasing glass. Push the ball of molten glass around the bead as far as it goes, aiming for one revolution (photo 3). Then, hold the bead slightly below the flame, and continue heating and applying molten glass to it. You'll use the firm part of the rod

as a tool to push the glass around the bead and cover the frit.

As you work your way around the bead, lightly push the molten glass into the edge of the previously applied glass to completely cover the bead. Continue encasing until

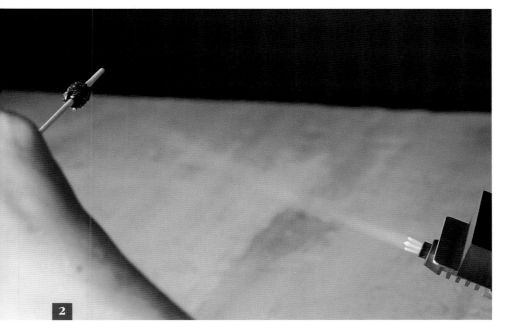

2

4

Your first attempts at covering aventurine will probably result in an uneven layer of glass, but you can correct this. Hold the bulk of the bead just beneath the flame while you turn the bead and heat the top layer to molten. This position in the lower part of the flame keeps the bead's interior slightly cooler and firmer. Thus, it is less likely to distort when you're trying to move the encasing glass. Use a graphite paddle or marver to reshape the bead, even out the encased layer as needed, or finish the ends (photo 5). The finished bead shows how the aventurine sparkles through the clear glass, creating a beautiful effect (photo 6).

5

6

AVENTURINE CHUNK:
Aventurine chunk is used to make stringers that can be added to your beads. You'll encase aventurine in clear glass before pulling it. You can use aventurine stringers to decorate beads in most of the ways previously described, although they don't work very well for making dots. Gold and blue aventurine will consistently pull into smooth stringers, but green aventurine can sometimes result in uneven ones.

Chunk comes in various sizes that range from around the size of a tennis ball to a pea. If you buy larger pieces of chunk, you can break them up into smaller ones with a chisel. (Take safety measures when you do this, such as covering the chunk with a cloth and wearing protective glasses.) It is sold by weight, and you can vary the sizes of the pieces in the batch that you buy. If you're working with pieces of chunk any larger than about the size of a regular grape, you'll need to preheat them in the kiln before using them. Smaller pea-sized pieces can be heated at the torch.

Preheat larger chunks to 970°F/521°C in the kiln. This will decrease the likelihood of thermal shock. After the chunk is heated, heat the end of a transparent rod to molten. Quickly reach inside the kiln with it, and press the molten glass onto the chunk. It will stick to the preheated chunk. Bring the chunk out of the kiln and into the cooler part of the flame.

If you're using smaller pieces of chunk, use the molten end of a glass rod to pick them up from a marver. Use the rod as your holding tool, and bring the chunk into the cooler part of the flame. Heat it

until it's molten (photo 7). Keep it in this part of the flame to avoid burning the aventurine. As the chunk softens, roll it on a marver or paddle to shape it so that it becomes round and forms an end on the transparent glass rod.

Next, heat the end of a second clear rod to molten. At the same time, keep the shaped aventurine warm in the end of the flame. Encase the aventurine with clear molten glass as described in the section on encasing glass rod to make stringers (see page 63). Smooth the encased section by rolling it on a marver or paddle (photo 8, next page). Make certain to cover any open spots so that the aventurine doesn't migrate to the surface.

After you've encased and smoothed the aventurine on the end of the rod, allow it to cool slightly and firm up. Depending on the length of the encased section, reheat a small portion of it to molten and pinch the end with tweezers, pulling the molten combination of glasses into a stringer. You'll probably get several pulls from the molten mass.

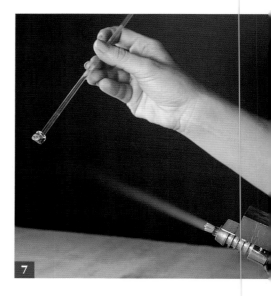

7

AVENTURINE FILIGRANA

RODS: Blue and copper (often called gold) aventurine is available in premade rod form. The most commonly used is filigrana, which is aventurine encased in clear glass. An alternative to this is clear glass encased with aventurine. These rods can be used to make beads or pulled into stringers, just like other glass rods. However, when you pull them, the particles thin out and become less intense and glittery. If you prefer a very bright aventurine stringer for decorating your bead, you'll need to make the stringer yourself from chunk.

Aventurine filigrana tends to thermal shock quite easily, even when very slowly heated at the torch or preheated in a kiln. When you're ready to use it to make a stringer or a bead, heat it very slowly in the cooler part of the flame.

The alternative rod with aventurine on top of clear can be purchased pre-annealed. Therefore, it will suffer less from thermal shock. This rod is more expensive and subject to burning since it isn't encased in clear glass.

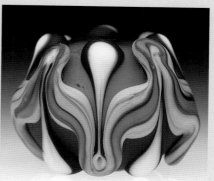

Top left: Inara Knight
Inner Fire, 2001
3.8 x 3.2 x 0.95 cm
Lampworked, wound, and flattened; soft dichroic glass; surface trailing and frit
Photo by artist

Top right: Andrea Land
Nouveau Arabesque, 2003
2 x 2.7 x 2.7 cm
Lampworked; soda-lime glass; encased in transparent colors; handmade cane and dots; raked and lightly etched
Photo by Scott Smudsky

Center: Harlan Simon
Flame Harlequins, 2003
2 x 2 x 1 cm each
Layered dots; soda-lime glass; clear cased finish
Photo by Richard Reed

Bottom: Daniel Adams
Offset Eye Beads, 2004
8 x 2 x 2 cm to 12 x 2 x 2 cm
Lampworked; soda-lime glass
Photo by Roger Schreiber

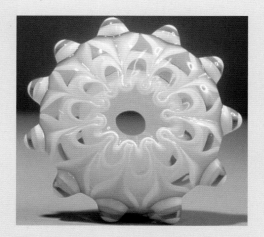

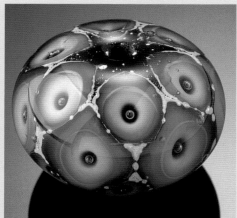

Top left: Brad Pearson
Snowflake Series Bead, 2003
1.5 x 5 cm
Lampworked; soda-lime glass; pulled dots
raked to form radiating pattern
Photo by artist

Top center: Tom Holland
Untitled, 2001
2.8 x 2.8 x 1.7 cm
Lampworked; dots
Photo by artist

Top right: Marjorie Langston
Untitled, 2004
3.8 x 3.8 x 1.6 cm
Soda-lime glass; raked and stacked dots
Photo by Art Image Studio

Center left: Brad Pearson
Cosmos Series Bead, 2003
2.7 x 3 cm
Lampworked and encased; soda-lime glass;
silver leaf
Photo by Taylor Dabney

Center right: Debby Weaver
Blue Feathered Ribbon Bead, 2002
3 x 2 cm
Lampworked; soft Italian glass; layered and
raised dots
Photo by T.R. Wailes

Bottom: Robin Foster
Purple Pleiades Plus Two, 2003
1.5 to 3.5 cm
Soda-lime glass; striking of ruby glass with
repeated heating and cooling
Photo by David Orr

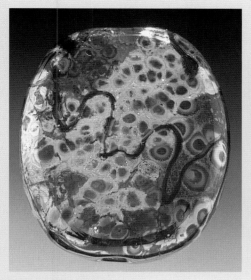

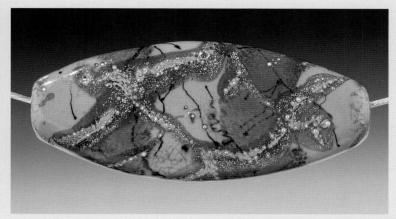

Top left: Louise Mehaffey
Blue Moss, 2004
3.7 x 3.2 x 1 cm
Lampworked; soda-lime glass; copper and
silver leaf, enamel, and reduction frit
Photo by Jerry Anthony

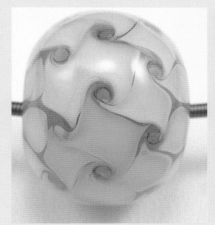

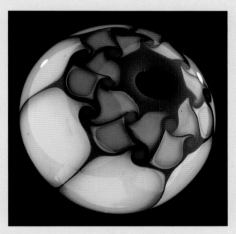

Top right: Sandra Saylor Seaman
Earth & Air Enamel Tab, 2003
2.2 x 4 x 0.9 cm
Soft glass; enamel powders, gold aventurine,
and silver foil
Photo by artist

Center left: Marjorie Langston
Untitled, 2004
1.6 cm diameter
Soda-lime glass; stacked and twisted dots
Photo by Art Image Studio

Center right: Terri Caspary Schmidt
Segmented Amber Pod, 2000
2.1 x 2.5 cm
Lampworked and layered; soda-lime glass;
twisted-dot end details
Photo by David Egan

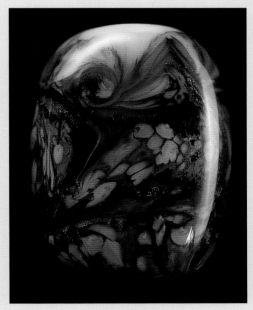

Bottom left: Kimberly Rogers
Landscape Strata, 2002
3 x 2.5 x 1.25 cm
Lampworked; soda-lime glass; enamels,
frit application, and cased
Photo by Jack Dewitt

Bottom right: Budd Mellichamp
Multicolor Iridized Swirl, 2001
1.3 x 0.8 cm
Lampworked; raked pattern; iridized;
moretti glass
Photo by Rob Overton

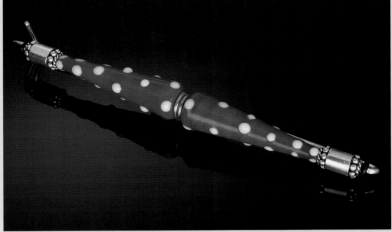

Top left: Michelle Waldren
Ribbon Cane Disk and Teardrop, 2003
8.9 x 2.5 cm (left); 7.6 x 7.6 cm (right)
Lampworked and layered; soda-lime glass;
ribbon cane
Photo by Roger Shrieber

Top right: Laura Lubin
Red and White Brooch, 2003
6.4 x 1.3 cm
Lampworked; soda-lime glass and
sterling silver
Photo by Steve Gyurina

Center: Laura Lubin
Three Beads, 1999
2.5 x 2.5 cm each
Lampworked; opalino glass
Photo by Paul Avis

Bottom: Heather Trimlett
Pinwheel Beads, 2002
3.8 x 0.6 cm each
Lampworked; soda-lime glass
Photo by Melinda Holden

Top left: Amy Johnson
Counting, 2003
41.9 x 2.5 x 3.2 cm
Lampworked; soda-lime glass; dots
Photo by Peter Tang

Top center: Sage
Watcher/Mask, 1999
4.4 x 3.1 x 0.9 cm
Lampworked; soda-lime glass; murrini,
dots, and feathered lines
Photo by Tom Holland

Top right: Hiroko Hayashi-Kogure
Kotsudumi, 2003
1.7 x 2.8 x 1.7 cm
Lampworked; soda-lime glass; twistie, dots,
and raked gold foil
Photo by artist

Center: Martha Giberson
Tribute, 2000
61 x 3.8 cm (necklace)
Lampworked; soda-lime glass and sterling
silver beads; stringers
Photo by Steve Gyurina

Bottom: Brad Pearson
Assorted Beads, 2004
1 to 4 cm diameter
Lampworked; soda-lime glass
Photo by Taylor Dabney

Now that you've worked your way through the basics of beadmaking—both shaping and simple decoration—you can add more techniques to your repertoire. You can combine or layer these treatments, giving you more possibilities for enhancement.

For example, using enamels greatly expands your color palette, and reduction frits and metals give you more surface choices. Non-glass materials such as mica powder, baking soda, and etching solution can be used to alter the bead's texture. In this chapter, we'll also cover intermediate shaping techniques to prepare you for the advanced techniques in chapter 5.

Applying Enamels

Enamel is very finely ground glass that is commonly applied to metal. Certain enamels are compatible with soft glass and can be used on beads. Enamels are available in a broad range of colors through beadmaking suppliers, and they broaden your color choices for beads considerably. A thin layer can either intensify the bead's color or create a new color, while dusting the surface will create a speckled effect.

Enamels will melt but not blend into one another, so you can't combine two colors to make a new one. And, since the enamel coating is thin, you can engrave through the surface with a tool to create designs and show a layer of color underneath. Applying them is fairly simple, while the possible design variations are endless. This section explains some of the most effective ways to use enamels.

Full Coverage

If you wish to completely cover a bead with enamel, make the core bead from a glass color close to that of the enamel. Fill a spoon with the enamel, and place it on a small plate within easy reach of your non-dominant hand. Shape the bead and heat it to a dull orange. Hold the enamel underneath the flame and lower the bead into it, rolling it back and forth until the whole surface is coated (photo 1).

Lift the bead back up into the cooler part of the flame, and turn it to heat the whole bead (photo 2). As the enamel melts, the surface will change from a textured one that resembles an orange peel to a smooth and glossy one. Since enamel has a lower melting point than soft glass, heat the enamel carefully so it doesn't burn. If it burns, it will turn light gray.

If you want to add more enamel to your bead, apply more coats in the same way. You may need as many as three coats to get complete cov-erage. After this is done, you can further decorate the bead with dots, stringers, frit, or other applications. Since you have now coated the bead with a thin layer of glass, be careful about the amount of heat that you apply to the bead when you decorate it.

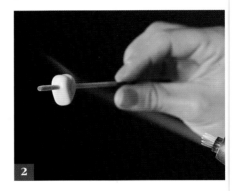

Enameled Stringers

To make enameled stringers that can be used to decorate beads, heat the end of a glass rod to molten before rolling it in enamel (photo 3). Carefully melt the enamel onto the glass rod so that it doesn't burn. Add at least three layers of enamel, melting each in separately. Pull the glass out into a stringer (photo 4).

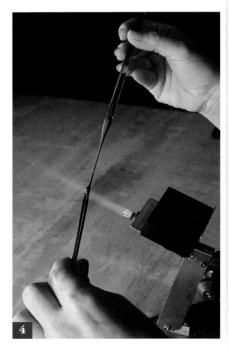

> **NOTE**
>
> *When you apply the enameled stringer to a bead, do so in the cooler part of the flame to prevent it from burning. To protect the enamel from burning when you apply it to a bead, you can encase it before pulling it into a stringer, if you wish.*

Enameled Patterns

You can use various tools to create enameled patterns on beads. A simple way to do this is to sift the enamel out in a thin layer on a marver (photo 5). before pulling a comb or fork through it (photo 6). Heat a bead to a dull orange glow, and roll it in the powder to pick up the pattern (photo 7). Melt the enamel onto the bead as described previously.

Another option is using a piece of paper punched with a design to apply enamel. A variety of paper punches are available at craft supply stores. Place the punched design face-down on the marver, and use a sifter to sprinkle a light, even layer of enamel over the shape (photo 8). Carefully lift up the paper to leave the design on the marver (photo 9). Roll the hot bead over the design (photo 10).

You can also use a rasp as a marver for this purpose. Sprinkle enamel in the recessed areas of the file, and roll or press a heated bead over the ridges to pick up the powder (photo 11).

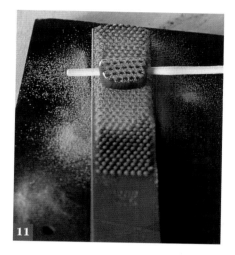

5

8

6

9

7

10

Boiled Enamel

Boiling enamels on the bead's surface creates a variegated appearance. Begin by rolling a bead in one or more enamel colors. You can completely cover the bead with a variety of colors. You can also sprinkle them on in patches with a sifter, or pick up bits of color from a marver.

Carefully melt the enamels into the bead's surface in the cooler part of the flame. Then move the bead close to the tips of the cones in the flame (photo 12). The enamel will begin to bubble and boil very quickly. Rotate the bead in the flame, boiling either the whole surface or patches of applied color. Boiling the enamel will leave an uneven, textured surface that can be left as it is, or smoothed out on a marver.

Sifted Enamel

To create a speckled surface, lightly sift the enamel onto a bead. To do this, hold the sifter over a very hot bead and scrape your thumbnail up and down the shaft of the handle to vibrate it slightly, releasing a light and even layer of powder while rotating the bead (photo 13). Melt this layer into the surface so that it's smooth, or leave it in the flame less time to create a textured look that resembles an orange peel.

To create a chunky, sand-like effect, you can heat the enamel differently. Position the bead beneath the

cooler portion of the flame, and move it up so that only the enamel is heated (photo 14). The lower melting point of the enamel will cause it to melt into itself, making the bead look rough and aged.

Engraved Enamel

After you've annealed your bead, it's possible to scratch through a light layer of enamel on the surface to create patterns and reveal the

bead's color underneath. Use an engraving tool or a small hand-held drill with a diamond-embedded tip. Leave the bead on its mandrel, using it as a handle to control the bead while you engrave it.

Enamel Paint

You can use enamel paint (finely ground enamels mixed with water, oil, or acrylic-based medium) and a small brush to paint details and designs on the surface of a bead. Mix the enamels yourself or buy premixed paints from a glass or clay supplier.

To make this painting easier, paint enamels on a surface that's been lightly sifted with regular enamel. If you wish, use enamel that matches the bead's color and is barely noticeable. Heat the enamel to the orange-peel stage. The textured surface created by the enamel makes it easier to discharge the paint.

Paint on a cold, annealed bead that is still on its mandrel. Use the mandrel as a handle while you paint. Once you've painted the bead, place it in a cold kiln, making sure it doesn't touch the kiln floor or another bead. Raise the temperature to 1150°F (621°C) to make sure that the paint fuses with the bead's surface. As soon as the kiln reaches this temperature, vent it to bring it back down to annealing temperature. The bead can slump if allowed to linger at the higher temperature for more than 10 minutes. Lowering the temperature quickly will prevent this.

Glass That Changes in the Flame

The following section covers several types of glass that can be altered in the flame, either by changing the balance of oxygen and propane or through the use of extreme heat. By using *reduction frit,* you can coax a metallic response on the bead's surface. *Anice white* is white, soft glass that changes when exposed to a reduction flame. *Intense black glass* spreads out on the surface of a bead to create a lacy, web-like look when a lot of heat is applied. These glasses can be used in combination with others for interesting results.

Reduction Frit

The process of *reduction* refers to a type of flame chemistry in which the amount of oxygen is reduced in proportion to propane, producing what is known as a reduction flame with a reduction atmosphere. Reduction can only be accomplished reliably with a duel-fuel torch.

Reduction frit is made from glass that reacts chemically in a reduction atmosphere. The lack of oxygen in the flame causes metallic oxides in the glass to surface, producing a shiny metallic finish that is sometimes compared with raku.

Reduction frit has a different COE than soft glass. Therefore, frit should only be used as a thin layer on the surface of a bead to reduce the possibility of the bead cracking as a result of incompatibility. Reduction frit comes in various sizes, from powder to larger chunks. Avoid using larger chunks, however, because they can add too much glass to the surface, raising the risk of the bead cracking.

The bead's color will affect how the reduction frit looks. Dark colors show the metallic effect very well.

Also keep in mind that some glass colors will reduce when exposed to the reduction flame. The results may surprise you!

Working with Frit in a Reduction Flame

Apply reduction frit to a hot bead by picking it up from a spoon, small dish, or marver before melting it into the bead. A small amount goes a long way, since the frit has a tendency to spread considerably on the bead's surface. Before putting the frit into a reduction flame, heat the bead to a dull orange glow in a neutral flame so that the bead's surface is molten.

Next, work with the flame to create a reduction atmosphere. You can do this one of two ways: Turn up the amount of propane to reduce the proportion of oxygen to propane, so that the flame is large, bushy, and orange (photo 1). Or turn down the amount of oxygen. When you do this, the

cones of the flame will soften and elongate (photo 2).

Hold the bead in the flame for a few seconds and take it out to see if reduction has occurred. When it happens, you'll see the bead change as the metals move to its surface, creating a metallic or iridescent quality. If more time is needed to achieve this effect, put the bead back in the flame.

You can vary the response of the frit in a reduction atmosphere by changing the mix of oxygen to propane, by holding it in the flame for shorter or longer periods of time, or by varying the temperature of the bead when placed in the flame.

If you aren't pleased with the reduction effect, it's possible to reverse the process and try again. Bring your flame back to neutral and reheat the bead. The metallic look will go away. You can reverse the effect several times, but too many times can burn the frit and turn it gray.

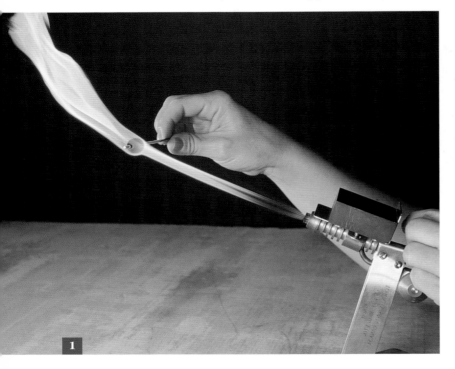

1

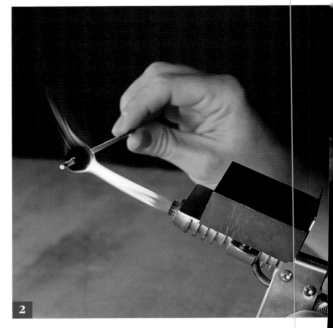

2

Reduction Stringers

You can also pull reduction stringers that can be dotted or wrapped on the bead before being put into the reducing flame. Powdered or fine frit will give you the best results.

To make a reduction stringer, begin by heating the end of a glass rod to molten, and then apply the frit (photo 3). Melt the frit until it evens out. Apply a second layer and melt it. Pull the molten end out into a stringer.

3

Anice White Glass

Anice white is a type of white soft glass that can be coaxed to behave in an unusual way when exposed to a reducing flame. Rods of this glass tend to have a rough surface and are milky and less opaque than regular white rods.

This kind of glass is usually applied in stringer form. Heat the rod to molten in a neutral flame, and pull a thick stringer. Once you've pulled the glass into a stringer it will be smooth and therefore difficult to tell apart from regular white stringers. For this reason, keep a nice white stringer separate from other white stringers.

To decorate a bead with the stringer, use a neutral flame. After you've added as much of the stringer as you wish, change the flame to a reducing one by turning up the propane until the flame elongates and turns orange and bushy. Melt the stringer into the bead's surface and wait for the reaction to take place (photo 4). The stringer will develop a dark line along the length of it.

4

This effect can be intensified somewhat by changing the flame back to a neutral one and heating the bead's surface until it's very hot, keeping the interior firm so that the bead doesn't become misshapen. To do this, hold the bead slightly below the flame while heating it.

You can add other colors to the bead along with anice white. However, when the bead is exposed to the reducing flame, the other colors may respond and undergo reduction in their own way.

Intense Black Glass

Black rods available in soft glass are actually composed of a very dark purple. Even though they look black, you can see that they're slightly transparent and purple when you pull them into stringers.

In contrast, intense black glass rod in stringer form is an opaque, true black. A surface effect, generally known as *black web* or *black lace*, is created when you use this black, since it has a tendency to deteriorate when exposed to a lot of heat and a slightly *oxidizing flame*.

Using intense black stringers to create a special effect on a bead works better with some glass colors than with others. Lighter opaque colors, such as ivory, purple, pea green, teal green, and coral, work very well, as do some transparent colors. Some *striking colors*, such as red and orange, don't work well. Experiment with your favorite colors and see what happens.

To use intense black, heat the end of a rod of it to molten. Pull out a very thin, almost hair-like stringer, since a little bit goes a long way (photo 5). Now wind a bead of any length without too much concern about the final shaping. If you wish, add other colors to the bead. These colors don't need to be put down in an exact pattern. Add the intense black stringer in a random pattern, while trying to distribute it evenly (photo 6).

Adjust the flame so that it's oxidizing (or has more oxygen than a neutral one). To do this, turn the oxygen valve *toward* you in a counterclockwise motion. The cones at the end of the flame will grow shorter and become sharper looking. The torch will also make a louder hissing sound.

Heat the bead in this flame until it glows a bright orange. The colors and black stringer will melt into the surface of the bead, and the glass will draw away from the ends of the bead towards the center. The intense black will begin to break down and spread out into tiny

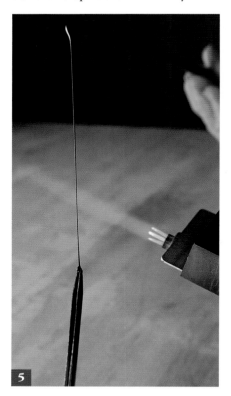

threads (photo 7). When you're happy with the effect, take the bead out of the flame (photo 8).

Because the bead has been exposed to so much heat, the ends will probably need reshaping. To do this, use a neutral flame.

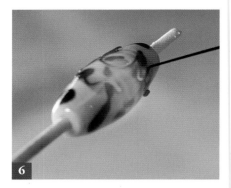

Encasing Beads

You can encase, or enclose, an entire bead with a layer of clear or transparent glass, or you can encase individual elements that you've added to a bead. The addition of glass over part of the bead will magnify, and thus enhance, whatever is underneath it.

Learning to encase successfully takes some practice. One of the main challenges is learning to apply glass without trapping air bubbles that are large enough to show up in your work later. You must also be careful to apply glass that is clean and free of any burned areas, since such flaws will interfere with the effect and clarity of the glass.

Many of the applications that we'll describe in the next sections (such as mica powder or silver shavings) can be enhanced through encasing. Encased layers over the whole bead can create an amazing illusion of depth.

We've already discussed encasing a bead covered with aventurine (see page 74). This technique also works well for encasing a fairly smooth bead with a relatively thick layer of glass. This section

> **NOTE**
>
> *If you're doing a lot of encasing, it's a good idea to use a thicker rod of glass, since it contains more interior glass that is clean. Some beadmakers spend a lot of time washing their clear glass very carefully in the beginning while others spend more time skimming the rod while it's hot. As you work with encasing, you'll discover a balance between these techniques that works well for you.*

introduces you to other, more advanced methods of encasing.

To prepare clear or transparent rods for encasing, wash them and wipe them down with rubbing alcohol so they're as clean as possible. Do this every time you begin to use the glass. As you heat the glass, check it for impurities or any dirt that wasn't cleaned away. Use pointed tweezers to pluck out and skim off any imperfections while the glass is very molten, instead of trying to remove debris from the bead later.

To encase individual elements on a bead, such as fine silver wire or a slice of millefiori, take the bead out of the flame and cool it until it isn't glowing. This cooling will keep the designs from distorting. Heat a clear rod to molten so that it's very hot and soft, and touch the molten glass down on the desired spot. Lift the rod away from the bead slightly and separate the glass in the flame. If you intend to cover several elements on a bead, work your way around the bead while keeping the whole thing warm. If needed, use a thinner rod for small areas.

To encase the entire bead, you can use the technique already described, or try one of the following. Practice each and see what works best for you.

To encase a bead with a thinner layer of glass, heat the clear rod to very molten, so that it's almost dripping off the rod. Hold a cooled bead (no longer glowing) beside and slightly beneath the flame, and push the molten glass down the length of it. You can stripe the glass straight down the length of the bead, similar to encasing a glass rod for making a stringer or partially wrap it around and down the length (photo 1). Notice the angle of the rod in the photo. The angle at which you hold the firm portion of the rod helps to push the molten glass onto the bead. Additionally, pushing very molten glass onto or around the bead is less likely to trap air bubbles than wrapping glass around it.

Another encasing technique involves heating a larger amount of glass to very molten before flattening it into a paddle shape. You can do this by pressing the glass with a graphite paddle on a marver, or you can compress it with a parallel press (photo 2).

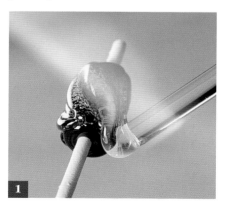

NOTE

Generally, it's a good idea to avoid bubbles in the glass so that it's as clear as possible. However, in some cases, bubbles can be added purposefully to enhance a design, as on a bead that has an aquatic theme.

To encase the bead, reheat the paddle to molten, and wrap it around the bead (photo 3). Disconnect the glass rod and smooth the glass on a marver or with a graphite paddle. If a significant portion of the bead hasn't been covered with the first paddle of glass, make and add another one. Try using a larger diameter of rod to make a larger paddle, if needed. Cover any smaller uncovered areas with molten glass directly from the rod.

When the entire bead has been covered, check for spots that you may have missed, and cover them with additional hot glass. The bead will probably be bumpy at this point. Hold the bead slightly below or above the flame so that it hits only the clear layer, allowing the interior to stay firm so that your designs don't get distorted (photo 4).

As the clear layer softens, smooth it out with a paddle, or roll it on a marver. You can use tweezers to move a small amount of glass to an uncovered area (photo 5). Check to see that the glass is even all the way around. This process might take awhile, so be patient as you heat the surface and paddle it carefully.

Altering Bead Surfaces with Non-Glass Materials

Baking Soda

After you've finished shaping and decorating a bead, you can use simple baking soda to alter a bead's surface. Rolling the bead in soda creates a matte, rough surface. You can also add baking soda to selective areas so that the matte finish contrasts with shinier parts.

To use baking soda, place enough of it in a shallow bowl to make a mound, and heat the bead to a dull orange glow before rolling the bead in it (photo 1). Place the bead in the cooler part of the flame, turn it, and watch the reaction happen (photo 2). The surface of the bead will bubble and become pocked. Add more soda and heat the bead again if you want to increase the effect.

This section covers ways to change the bead's surface by applying baking soda, mica powders, or etching solution. These materials respond to and affect the surface of the glass—sometimes while it is still hot and sometimes after it has cooled. Baking soda etches the glass so that it resembles organic-looking beach glass, while etching solution lends an even and soft appearance to the glass. Mica powders add color and iridescence, creating some surprising responses, depending on the combination of the base bead and the color of the mica.

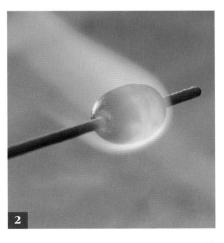

Mica Powders

Mica powders (pixie dust) are superfine powders composed of mica and colorants. These compounds lend a lustrous, metallic look to the bead. The darker the bead, the more the powders will contrast with the original color.

To use mica powder, place it in a spoon, or a small bowl made of an inflammable material, such as glass or metal. After you've finished shaping a bead, roll it in the powder while it has a dull orange glow (photo 4).

Warm the bead in the cooler end of the flame (photo 5). Heat it carefully since the dust is very sensitive to heat and can burn out easily. After you're done, allow the bead to cool slightly before cooling or annealing it.

You can also encase mica powders or pixie dust with transparent glass to create a different effect. When you add a layer of clear glass, the powders will thin out, and the color of the base bead will show through more. The clear layer will also magnify the mica.

Before you encase the bead, remove as much of the gathered dust as possible, since the glass won't stick to the bead if the pow-der is too thick. You can simply shake off some of the dust, or remove the excess by rolling the bead very quickly on a damp cloth. Then encase the bead as you would aventurine frit. When encasing the bead, keep it below the flame as much as possible to avoid burning the powder.

3

In addition to these options, you can apply clear or transparent stringers or trail glass on top of mica powder. Fuse the glass that you apply to the mica bead very carefully to avoid burning the powders.

Mica powder is very pervasive and spreads easily, so consider using a separate set of tools to work with it. It's also a good idea to use a designated crock-pot filled with vermiculite for cooling the coated beads. Or always put them directly into the kiln to keep the dust from migrating to other beads. When you take the annealed beads out of the kiln, wipe off the extra powder with a damp rag or paper towel before putting them in water.

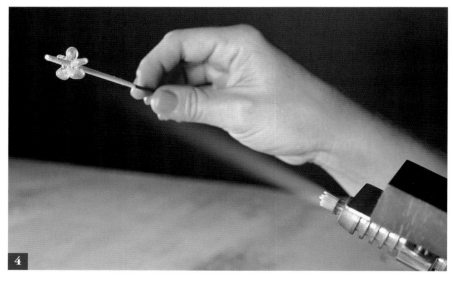

4

Etching

After it has cooled, you can etch the surface of a bead by bathing it with etching fluid or painting smaller areas with etching cream. The cream takes longer to process.

Etching works well on pale transparent colors, but it can also be used to brighten a bead that has darkened areas of reduction, which is more likely to happen if you reduce or overheat opaque turquoise or teal green.

Etching cream is painted on the bead to create designs. Before you do this, anneal the bead on the mandrel and leave it intact. After painting on the desired design, allow the cream to process as recommended by the manufacturer. Remove the bead from the mandrel after you rinse it off, and check it to make sure you've got the effect you want.

To etch with fluid, pour it into a large plastic container, so that the beads can be suspended without touching the sides of the container. String the cleaned, annealed beads

5

> **NOTE**
>
> *Etching beads with fluid is fairly simple, but you should follow some precautions when using it. Although ammonium bifloride, the solution used to etch soft glass, is much milder than other etching solutions, it should still be handled with great care. Wear rubber gloves and eye protection when working with the fluid and don't use metal tools, since the acid will corrode them.*

on monofilament line and lower them into the fluid (photo 6). Let them process for the amount of time recommended by the manufacturer.

If you plan to etch a large number of beads at once, pour the solution into a small salad or herb spinner. Lower the beads into the inner strainer, and allow them to process in the solution. Spin the beads gently every few minutes to move them around and expose all the areas to the acid. When you aren't processing beads, return the acid to its original container.

If you want to mask off parts of the bead so that areas remain shiny in contrast to the etched ones, such as millefiori canes or other decoration, paint on a resist such as colored nail polish, white glue, or hot wax (photo 7). If you use nail polish or glue, let it dry completely before lowering the beads into the solution. If you use wax, melt it in a pan on a hot plate, and then lower the bead into it to coat it. After the wax hardens, use a craft knife to carve away the areas to be etched.

After the masked beads have soaked for the appropriate time, lift them out of the etching solution, and place them in a container filled with 2 cups ($\frac{1}{2}$ L) of water and a small amount of baking soda. The soda will act as a neutralizer. Swirl the beads in this solution, then rinse them in clear water and allow them to dry. The beads won't look etched until they dry. Remove the polish with polish remover, peel off the glue, or scrape off the excess wax before placing the beads in hot water to soften and remove the remaining wax.

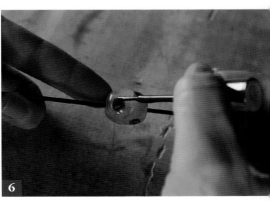

6

Intermediate Shaping and Sculpting Techniques

There are many possibilities for shaping and sculpting glass beads. As you become more comfortable working at the torch with molten glass, you can add detailed shaping. You'll use some familiar tools, such as a graphite paddle or marver, but you'll also use some new tools to shape, such as a knife-edged tool or scissors.

Creating Furrows

You can alter the shape of a bead by making grooves in it with a knife-edged graphite paddle, a single-edged razor blade in a pin vise, or a sharp-edged putty knife.

After the bead has been shaped and decorated, allow it to cool until it no longer glows. Adjust the flame until it's smaller and more concentrated but make sure the mix of gases is still correct. With this narrower flame, heat a strip along the length of the bead.

Bring the bead out of the flame and push the edge of your tool into the heated area (photo 1). Continue to work around the bead, heating a strip at a time before creating each furrow (photo 2). You can place furrows parallel to the mandrel, or cut them at an angle to create a winding effect on the finished bead.

Because using graphite or metal tools to make furrows can create stress in the bead, you must reheat the bead evenly in the cooler part of the flame until it is a dull orange before putting it away to cool.

Cutting Hot Glass

You can also shape a hot bead by cutting it with a pair of scissors to create different shapes. Use heavy scissors with metal handles. Choose a pair that's long enough to keep your hands a safe distance from the hot glass, such as kitchen shears.

In the beginning, try working with a disc bead. After you wrap the bead, straighten and smooth the sides and allow the bead to cool a bit. Heat one side of the disc to a dull orange glow and bring it out of the flame. Snip the glass, cutting all the way through it (photo 3). Don't cut too close to the mandrel since this might loosen the release. Heat subsequent areas, and continue to cut a design as you work your way around the bead. Five or more cuts will lend the bead a floral look. You can use tweezers, pliers, or a stringer to shape and move the petals to create the look you want.

Sculpting with a Graphite Paddle

A graphite paddle can be used to do finer shaping on a bead. A very basic way to learn about this is by making a heart-shaped bead from a round, flattened bead. (More advanced sculpting techniques will be covered in the next chapter.)

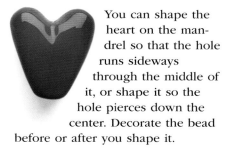

You can shape the heart on the mandrel so that the hole runs sideways through the middle of it, or shape it so the hole pierces down the center. Decorate the bead before or after you shape it.

To shape a heart with the sideways hole through the middle, warm one edge of the bead to a dull orange glow, and use a graphite paddle to shape one side of the bead to form half of the bottom of the heart (photo 4). Heat the other side and push from the opposite direction to shape a point at the bottom of the heart (photo 5). Heat the top edge of the bead and use a knife-edged paddle to push in the top of the heart (photo 6). Reheat the bead and flatten it so that the sides are parallel.

95

To create a heart with the hole running down through the center, heat the flattened bead, and use the paddle to angle the edges, forming the bottom on each side of the mandrel (photo 7). On the wider top part, add a bit of hot glass to each side to create the lobes (photo 8). Use the knife-edged paddle to shape the glass and create definition (photo 9). If you want to decorate a heart-shaped bead after you shape it, keep it cool so that it doesn't distort as you do this.

Pinching Glass with Tweezers

You can also add shaping to beads using tweezers to create flaps or fin-like shapes. Begin by using parallel mashers or a graphite paddle and marver to make a square-shaped bead (photo 10). Reheat a corner (photo 11). Then pinch it with tweezers (photo 12). Repeat and pinch the other three corners. You can leave the flaps parallel to the mandrel, or you can reheat them and twist them (photo 13).

Since the flaps have been cooled considerably by manipulating them with a cold tool, reheat the bead in the tip of the flame until the base of it warms to a dull orange glow to prevent it from cracking (photo 14).

7

8

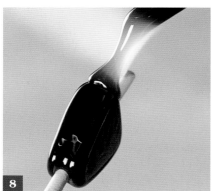

9

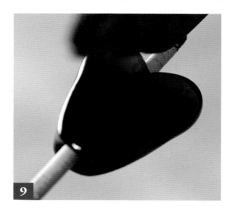

10

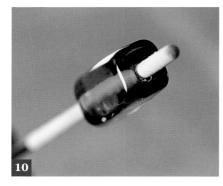

11

12

13

14

Making Large-Hole Beads

Large-hole beads can be incorporated into jewelry or are sometimes worn as rings. In this section, we'll describe how to make a simple, wide disc with a large hole, which will teach you the basics about this process.

Larger-diameter mandrels used to make these beads include steel welding rods that are available in various diameters up to $1/8$ inch (3 mm). Hollow steel tubing welded onto steel rods are used as even larger mandrels that reach up to $1^1/_2$ inches (3.8 cm) in diameter.

Working with larger mandrels takes some extra effort because you're working with a larger area of contact between the glass, the release, and the metal. The metal expands and contracts when heated and cooled, causing the release to break loose. The larger the mandrel is, the more this will happen. Therefore, briefly warm the mandrel in the specific area where you plan to wind the bead. It should reach an orange glow (photo 15). After this first warming, avoid hitting the mandrel directly with the flame, except when applying the first revolution of glass.

Allow the molten glass rod to lie down naturally on the mandrel without pushing it (photo 16). Hold the mandrel slightly below the flame as you continue to wind the softening glass around it.

Creating clean edges on any large-hole bead requires extra attention because the glass must be wrapped onto the mandrel very

evenly and straight. Due to its size, it will be more noticeable if you've veered off course while making the bead. Build up the glass as desired, building the bead taller than you wish the final bead to be. End the wrapping or building once you complete a revolution to help create an even bead.

Heat the glass in the flame so that it softens and settles onto the mandrel slightly. While you work, use a graphite paddle to push the glass as needed or straighten up the edges (photo 17).

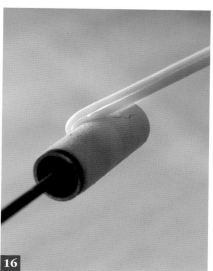

Since the interiors of these beads are larger, and thus more visible, it will take more time to clean them thoroughly. Generally, the surface will be rough, so try using steel wool to remove as much of the bead release as possible. If you want the bead to have a very clean and smooth surface, use a motorized rotary tool with a polishing/grinding bit to clean and smooth the interior. As you work, keep the bead wet by dipping it in and out of a bowl of water.

Adding Metals to Beads

The use and application of metals to beads creates a whole new range of possible designs. Metals can be applied to the surface using sheets of metal leaf or foil. Fine silver wire can be wrapped on like a stringer, and silver shavings can be rolled onto a bead to decorate it. Adding copper tubing to the inside a bead creates an intriguing look. The section that follows will explain how to incorporate all of these options.

Leaf

The basic application of silver, gold, and palladium leaf is the same, with the exception of copper, which is applied differently. We'll discuss these variations in this section.

To apply leaf, begin by pulling a sheet of it, with the surrounding papers, out of its book. These papers lend it support and keep you from touching it. Bend a corner of the top shoot up so it can be lifted easily in the next step.

Place the leaf and papers on a marver and weigh it down with a pair of tweezers. Tear or cut a piece of the leaf from the larger sheet, using the paper as support.

To apply leaf to a shaped bead, heat it to a dull orange glow. You can roll the hot bead on a piece of leaf to pick it up, or lift it up with tweezers and lay it down gently on the bead's surface (photo 1). Use the tweezers to burnish the leaf, making certain that all the leaf makes contact with the bead (photo 2). Return the bead to the cooler part of the flame to fuse the leaf (photo 3).

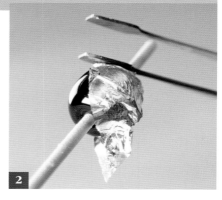

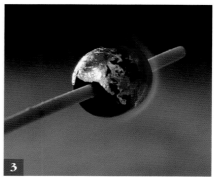

If you're using silver leaf, several effects are possible at the fusing stage. If you lightly heat the leaf, it will remain bright and silvery. If you leave it in flame longer, a portion of the silver will burn away, leaving an area stained with the silver. The color of the glass influences the silver stain. The addition of the leaf will cause some colors to look metallic and others iridized, while others will darken and yellow. All of these effects can be desirable, depending on the outcome you want. Experimentation is the key. Adding clear or transparent glass over the leaf in dot or stringer form creates another effect, preserving the silver at a certain stage. These areas contrast with those that are then burned away or change color.

In contrast to silver, gold leaf doesn't change color when it's applied to a bead. After the bead has been rolled on the gold leaf, burnish it, and put it back in a cooler part of the flame. Heat the bead gently until the gold softens and flows onto the surface (photo 4). Avoid the application of too much heat because this will cause the leaf to burn off, even if it is encased.

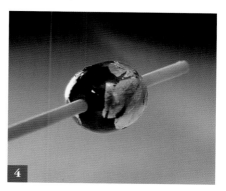

However, palladium can withstand a lot of heat, and it will change color when different amounts of heat are applied. It remains metallic even when exposed to intense heat, including the temperature needed for encasing. Palladium, however, is much more expensive than the other metals.

You can layer gold, silver, and palladium leaf on beads to create some very nice effects. The bead should already be shaped before you do this. The reaction of the metals with one another, the glass you use, and the amount of heat all contribute to different responses. Since gold leaf burns away quickly, you should add it last.

Copper leaf must be treated in a slightly different way than the other metals since it responds differently to the metal oxides in the glass. There are two ways to apply it. You can apply it directly to the glass. When using this method, white glass will show off the patina or blue-green color of the copper leaf. Copper leaf applied to ivory glass leaves a dark, variegated stain. When you roll the bead onto the leaf (photo 5) don't allow it to overlap, since those areas will leave a dark line when heated. Heat the bead in the flame until the leaf

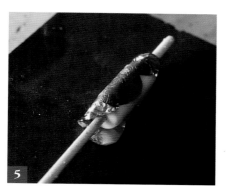

bubbles slightly and fuses to the surface of the glass (photo 6). When the glass cools slightly, you'll see the effect of the leaf. Our example shows this effect on white glass (photo 7).

6

7

Another way to apply copper leaf involves first sprinkling or rolling all or parts of a darker glass color in white or another light-colored enamel (photo 8). This background allows the copper to show up.

Copper leaf applied to sections of

8

99

enamel on a bead result in a patina, while the glass left free of enamel remains visible and, for the most part, unchanged.

After applying the enamel, heat it in the flame before rolling the bead on the copper leaf. Then burnish the leaf (photo 9). Return the bead to the flame and allow the copper to fuse (photo 10). The copper's appearance will vary with the enamel's color and the amount of time it's heated in the flame.

Foils

Metal foils are used and applied to beads in the same way as metal leaf. However, they're easier to manipulate because of their thickness. These metals react the same way in foil form as they do in leaf, with some slight differences. For instance, when silver foil is applied to a bead, it looks a bit heavier or spotted than silver leaf, and gold foil is less likely to disappear than gold leaf.

 Because foils have more body than leaf, they can easily be cut into decorative shapes to apply to beads. A wide variety of decorative punches available at craft supply stores can be used for this purpose. Choose from the smaller shapes for your beads.

Place a sheet of foil between two pieces of paper, such as notebook or printer paper, to provide support while you punch out the shapes. Carefully separate the foil pieces from the paper, and place them on a marver (photo 11). Roll a hot bead, glowing dull orange, over each shape that you wish to add (photo 12). Burnish each design with tweezers so the whole piece of foil makes contact with the glass. Return the bead to the flame to fuse the design onto it (photo 13).

Silver Leaf Stringers

To make a silvered stringer, heat about ½ inch (1.3 cm) of the end of a glass rod until it begins to slump. Roll the end of the rod over a sheet of silver leaf, wrapping it around the rod several times (photo 14). Bring the glass to molten in the flame, and then pull it out into a thick stringer. You can use this stringer to decorate beads as you would any other stringer, but keep in mind that silver will react differently with various colors. Try out various combinations to see what you like.

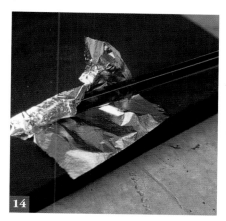

14

Silver Shavings and Fine Silver Wire

Silver shavings and fine silver wire can be added to a glass bead to create beautiful effects that differ from that of metal leaf or foil.

To add silver shavings to a bead, sprinkle them on a marver, and roll the hot bead in them (photo 15). The shavings will react with the hot glass in a way similar to leaf or foil, but the resulting surface will probably be rougher, depending on how the silver is picked up. Encasing the shavings with a transparent glass magnifies the silver and results in more color changes. And, of course, it gives your bead a smooth finish (photo 16).

15

16

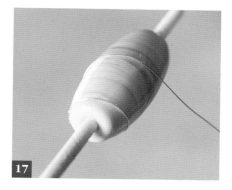

To apply silver wire to a bead, cut a long piece of wire (about 18 inches [45.7 cm] long). Bring the bead out of the flame, and touch the end of the wire down on it, allowing the silver to melt a bit and fuse to the bead. Con-tinue to wrap the wire around the bead (photo 17). Then place the bead very slowly back into the cooler part of the flame to fuse the silver, which will break up into a dotted line (photo 18). The more slowly you reheat the bead and fuse the wire, the cleaner and less broken the line will be; reheating it quickly will create a more broken, dotted line.

17

18

You can also add fine silver wire to beads by using pliers to shape short pieces of it into small shapes such as spirals or zigzags. Ideally, you should preheat these silver pieces on a torch marver or clean heated metal plate before applying them (photo 19).

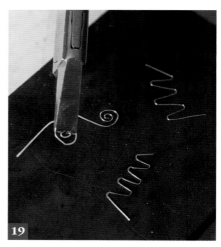

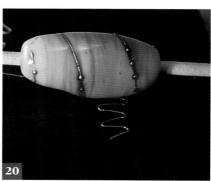

When you're ready to apply the silver designs, roll a very molten bead over one of the shapes to pick it up (photo 20). To fully attach the piece, you may need to push it with tweezers onto the bead's surface, just beneath the flame (photo 21) before returning it to the flame. If part of the wire isn't attached, it will ball up in the flame and distort the shape. When you return the bead to the cooler part of the flame, reheat the piece of wire very slowly (photo 22).

Since silver and glass are very different materials, the small bits of silver can easily fall off of the bead. For this reason, use a paddle or marver to push the silver into the bead's surface so that it is fused well. However, encasing the bead is really the only way to be certain that the silver will stay intact. Encasing also magnifies the silver.

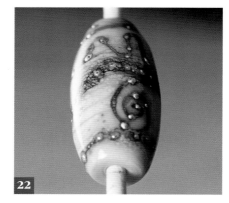

Copper Tubing

Copper tubing can be used as a decorative base for glass beads. When the tubing is heated and then covered with a clear or light transparent glass, the copper will glow intensely with a copper-red color inside the bead after it cools. You can use precut pieces made for beadmaking, or cut it yourself from a length of tubing. If you cut pieces, make sure to file the ends smooth before using them.

You can use coated or uncoated mandrels with copper tubing. Use an uncoated mandrel for smaller-

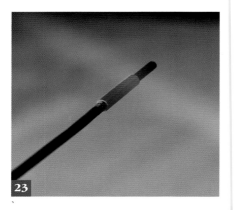

Making a Gravity Bead

diameter pieces of tubing. The mandrel must fit snuggly inside the copper tubing; or, if the mandrel's not quite large enough, bend it slightly to help hold the tubing in place. Preheat the tubing until it glows (photo 23, previous page). Begin laying down the glass on one end of it, and then wrap it around the tubing toward the opposite end (photo 24, previous page). When you wind the bead, avoid wrapping the glass onto the mandrel at each end of the tubing, since there's no bead release to keep it from sticking (photo 25).

Alternatively, you can use tubing that's large enough to slide over a mandrel coated in bead release. If you're using this method, wind the molten glass slightly over the end of the tubing onto the mandrel to hold it in place while you wind the bead. Wind the glass slightly over the other end as well. After you've finished wrapping the glass onto the tubing, you can add decoration to the bead's surface, if you wish.

25

Throughout the course of making beads, you've no doubt become very familiar with how the glass moves in the molten state. In chapter 2 you learned about gravity as a part of the beadmaking process.

Gravity can also be used to create colored patterns in beads. These beads are nicknamed "gravity beads." To make one, you'll apply color to a core bead before allowing gravity to help you move the color around. The movement of the flowing glass will remain in the cooled bead, creating an interesting pattern.

Since this technique exposes the glass to a lot of heat, keep the characterics of your glass colors in mind when choosing them for these beads—some will travel or spread out when heated.

This first example of a gravity bead uses stringers on a core barrel bead. To begin, pull a few thick stringers in colors of your choice. Set these aside while you make the core barrel bead.

Wind a long barrel-shaped bead, and smooth it into an even shape. Allow the bead to cool until the glow leaves it. Stripe a stringer down the bead's length (photo 1). Add two more stripes around the bead's circumference, dividing the bead into thirds. Use a bead

NOTE

Bring the bead out of the flame if the flow of the glass becomes too difficult to control, and allow the glass to cool off slightly before you begin again.

rake or a probe to push the ends of each stripe down close to, but not touching, the mandrel (photo 2).

Add a second stringer stripe next to the first, and push down the ends again. If you wish, add a third color in the same way (photo 3). Heat the bead until the stripes are fused well. Hold the bead in a horizontal position, and heat one end of it until it's very molten, rotating it away from you as you do this. Slow down the rotation of the bead until stripes of colored glass begin to flow toward you (photo 4).

Let the glass flow around this end of the bead. As you do this, you'll move the bead in and out of the flame, allowing it to cool a bit to help control the flow. The added stripes will flow into a swirled pattern around the end.

Now change the angle of the mandrel so that the glass flows toward the end to create an indentation. Bring the bead out of the flame to allow the glass to cool, and use the marver to lightly

shape the end and define it. Move to the opposite end and repeat this whole process, matching the two ends as much as possible (photo 5, previous page).

Next, work the center of the bead as you did the ends. Heat the glass to very molten, and allow the color to flow around the middle of the bead until you like the pattern (photo 6, previous page). When you're done, shape the bead with a marver or paddle.

An alternative to making a barrel bead is making a tall bead with various colors. Overlap several different colors of glass in a sporadic way to build up the bead. Then heat the bead until it's very molten. Allow the glass to flow down and wrap around the mandrel while you turn the bead and hold the mandrel at various angles, creating a symmetrical bead.

This technique is a test of your ability to control the flow of the glass while it's quite soft. Remember to simply bring the bead out of the flame if the molten glass becomes too difficult to control.

NOTE

In photos 5 and 6 on the previous page, notice the small hole drilled into the side of the paddle. This hole serves as a support for the tip of the mandrel.

Applying Millefiori

To add beautiful color and intricate design to your beads, you can apply premade canes. In chapter 5, you'll learn how to make your own simple canes from bundled glass, but these premade millefiori slices give you an opportunity to use more complex designs on your beads.

Always have extra slices of cane close to you as you're working, in case you drop one or a slice thermal-shocks during application. Use tweezers to pick up each piece of cane (photo 1).

To apply cane to a bead, begin by preheating a slice. This can be done in a kiln, on a hot plate, or simply by holding it with tweezers and passing it through the flame to

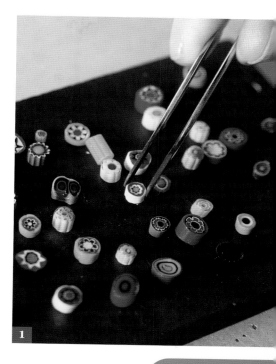

1

warm it up. If you use tweezers, be careful not to get the slice too hot, since the glass might stick to them.

Next, heat the base of the cane until it begins to glow (photo 1). On the bead, heat the area where you plan to place the cane slice until it glows a dull orange. Take the bead from the flame, and push the cane lightly into the bead (photo 2). Place the bead back in the flame.

When you apply cane to the bead's surface, and the cane is exposed to additional heat, it will begin to

spread out on the bottom and close up on the top. This makes the outside portion of the cane visible, and it also reduces the size of the inside image. To coax this response, continue to heat the top of the cane, allowing it to round off (photo 3). Give the whole bead a light bath of heat to warm it, and then pick up the next piece of cane. Use tweezers or a graphite paddle to center the cane as it melds with the bead (photo 4). The design of the cane will become slightly altered as it spreads out on the bead (photo 5).

If the cane has an interior design only, heat the area a bit more (so that it really glows), allowing you to push the cane deeper into the bead. Gently heat the cane, and use tweezers or a graphite paddle to coax the edges of the cane onto the bead so that the image stays open as the cane flattens (photo 6).

You can also keep the image open by applying a small amount of clear glass to the top of the cane after it's been pushed onto the bead, before giving it any more heat. This glass will keep the top of the cane from closing up when it's heated and settled into the bead, while also slightly magnifying the image (photo 7).

You can also choose to leave cane slices raised (not melted), and

encase them with glass. After the cane slice is attached to the bead, protect the top with a small dot of clear molten glass. After doing this, heat a large ball of clear glass until it's very molten (photo 8). Hold the molten glass above the bead, and allow it to flow onto the bead over the raised cane (photo 9) as well as other areas of the bead. Heat a ball of glass to apply to each raised cane, and allow it to flow over and fill in between canes.

The trick is to keep the slices firm and undistorted while covering them with very molten glass. Keep the base of the bead relatively cool. When all of the canes have been covered, use a graphite paddle to move and smooth the clear glass as needed. Use a knife-edge paddle to push areas of glass onto the bead's surface, as well as any undercuts that could trap air.

Working with Dichroic Glass

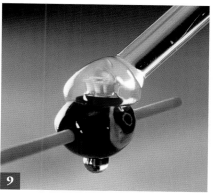

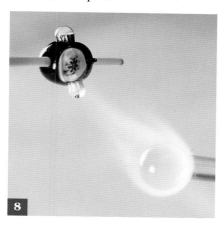

Decorating with beautiful dichroic glass can be slightly tricky, but the following section will help you find your way. The results are well worth the effort!

Soft-glass-compatible dichroic is available in two forms: Rods resembling a fat stringer, and sheets with a base of either clear or black glass. The sheet is usually sold in precut strips roughly ¹/₂ inch (1.3 cm) in width. Both versions can be applied to a bead as the finishing decoration or as a background for additional decoration.

Rods, both clear and black-based, work well as a simple wrap on a base bead (similar to a wrapped stringer). Dichroic sheet is usually used to cover most or all of a bead. If the sheet has black glass as its base, it is usually encased with clear glass to protect the dichroic coating.

Before beginning to apply dichroic, you must figure out which side of the glass contains the coating. On opaque (usually black) flat glass or glass rod, this side is fairly easy to determine because the coating reflects off of the base glass. If you're using textured glass, the dichroic coating is always on the textured side.

On sheets of flat dichroic glass that are clear-based, you can determine which side is coated by holding a shiny tool (such as tweezers) next to the surface so that you can see the tool's reflection. If the reflection touches the actual tool, it's the coated side. If there's a small separation between the tool and the reflection, the reverse side is coated.

Another way to determine which side is coated on a clear dichroic sheet is by holding the glass at an angle and looking at the edge to find the shimmering coating on one side. If you can see through the edge, the coating side is down. If you can't see through it, the coating side is up (photo 1).

Dichroic-coated rod, whether the base rod is clear or opaque, is coated on about half of the rod along the length of it with an uncoated section on each end, giving you a clear indication of what part of the rod has the coating.

Dichroic coating is vulnerable when exposed to the flame and oxygen, meaning it will burn and turn into unattractive scum. It can burn easily, so it needs to be treated carefully, with as little exposure to the flame as possible, even though some can't be avoided when working with it.

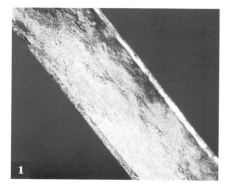

This problem is more prevalent when you're using a duel-fuel torch. This type of glass is actually easier to work with on a single-fuel torch, since there's less oxygen in the flame. If you're using a duel-fuel torch, work in the cooler part of the flame with a bit less oxygen.

To apply a layer of dichroic-coated opaque glass to a bead (either sheet or rod), the glass must be applied with the coating side up so that it can be seen. If you're using any kind of dichroic glass, you'll always aim the flame at the uncoated side of the glass.

To begin application, let your bead cool so that it's no longer glowing but is still hot. Heat the end of the rod or thin strip of sheet, and place it on the hot bead. Hold the bead beneath the flame with the rod or sheet pointing down through it, and the coated side facing you so that it isn't exposed to the flame (photo 2).

If you're working with dichroic rod, you can wrap it several times around the bead as a decoration. As you wrap it, be careful to keep the bead beneath the flame to prevent the coating from burning by exposing it directly to the flame. Make sure that the rod is heated and softened so that it fuses to the bead right away. When you've finished wrapping the bead, flame-cut the rod, as you would a stringer, moving a bit further out in the flame to avoid burning the coating.

Again, keep in mind that there's a delicate balance between melting the rod without burning it and getting it hot enough that it fuses. In general, it's best to keep dichroic glass out of the direct flame.

If you intend to further expose the bead to the flame, it's best to first encase the dichroic layer you've applied with clear glass to protect it from burning. As the encasing layer is added, keep the bead and coating away from the direct flame as much as possible.

If you're applying dichroic that's on a clear base, the base bead color will affect the color of the dichroic layer. Before making a bead, hold the dichroic glass over the rod you intend to use for the bead to get an idea of how they will look together.

Hold the base bead slightly above the flame with the dichroic rod or sheet beneath it. The coated side of the glass must face down and away from the direct flame (photo 3, next page). Once you've fused the edge of the dichroic to the bead, continue to heat the dichroic, and wrap it around the bead as it softens (photo 4, next page). As usual, keep the dichroic away from the direct flame as much as possible.

The dichroic coating will tend to wrap or crawl around the edge of the base glass. Use a paddle or tweezers to push the clear glass down to make contact with the base bead, trapping the coating. Do this continually as the glass softens and wraps around the bead (photo 5). Don't wait until all the dichroic has been wrapped onto the bead. This will be much easier to do with flat strip than with rod. On the rod, the coating will wrap around very quickly. Check to see that all edges of the applied glass are sealed down, including the area where the sheet may meet or slightly overlap.

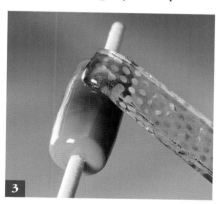

NOTE

You can add transparent colored stringers over the dichroic to change its appearance. Try out various combinations and see what you like.

It's important to avoid trapping air bubbles when working with strips of clear glass dichroic. The trapped air can get hot enough to burn the dichroic coating and create scum. Therefore, be sure that the base bead is smooth and has no ridges or indentations. Also, be sure to heat up the sheet until it's very molten so it fuses well to the base bead.

Once the dichroic has been sealed below the clear glass, additional decorations can be added to the bead. However, while doing this, work only with surface heat. If enough heat penetrates into the dichroic layer of the bead, the coating will thin out. If air is trapped within the coating, it will burn. Also, if the dichroic layer is allowed to get molten, the coating may break up or *craze*. Some beadmakers like this effect.

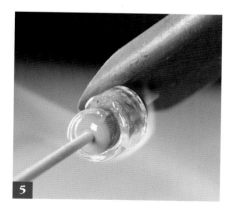

Top left: Laura Lubin
Turquoise Dichroic Bezel Earrings, 2003
2.5 x 1.3 cm each
Lampworked; dichroic glass and sterling silver bezel and wire
Photo by Steve Gyurina

Top right: Laura Lubin, *Black Sandblasted Pendant,* 2003
6.4 x 2.5 cm (pendant)
Lampworked; soda-lime glass and sterling silver; sandblasted
Photo by Steve Gyurina

Center left: Alethia Donathan, *Ginko Vessel,* 2003
3.8 cm
Lampworked and sandblasted; soda-lime glass; enamel,
gold, silver, and reduction frit
Photo by Azad

Center right: Alethia Donathan, *Seascapes,* 2003
3.5 x 2 cm
Lampworked; soda-lime glass; enamel and reduction frit
Photo by Azad

Bottom: Brad Pearson, *Glyph Series Beads,* 2003
2 x 2.9 cm each
Lampworked; soda-lime glass; masking technique using
overlapping dots and pixie dust
Photo by artist

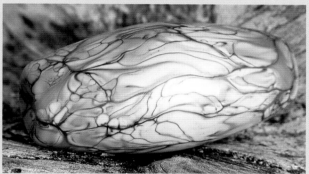

Top left: Karen Wojcinski, *Ice Beads,* 2003
1.5 cm diameter each
Soda-lime glass; dichroic layer, fine silver, dots, and casing
Photo by Jerry Anthony

Top right: Teresa Brittain
Hollow Bead with Powders and Leaf, 2003
1.9 x 3.2 cm
Lampworked; transparent soda-lime glass;
22-karat gold leaf, glass powders, and stringer
Photo by Robert Batey

Center: Travis Medak
Blue Lapidary Bead, 2004
4.5 x 2.5 cm
Lampworked; soda-lime glass; tumbled
Photo by artist

Bottom left: Alethia Donathan
River Rock Series, 2003
3.8 cm
Lampworked; soda-lime glass; enamel, copper,
silver, gold, and reduction frit
Photo by Azad

Bottom right: April Zilber, Untitled, 2000
3 x 2 x 0.5 cm
Lampworked; soda-lime glass; silver leaf
Photo by artist

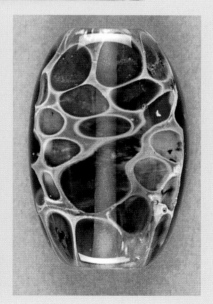

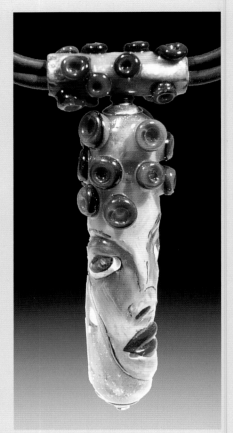

Top left: Emily McKillip
Reduction Frit Bicone, 2003
5.67 x 1.05 cm
Lampworked; soda-lime glass; reduction frit and stringer decoration
Photo by Dan Lobdell

Top right: Bronwen Heilman, *Sarah*, 2004
7.2 x 1.2 x 1.2 cm
Lampworked; soda-lime glass, sterling silver, copper, and rubber; enamel
Photo by artist

Center left: Kimberly Rogers
Dichroic Sphere, 2003
2.5 cm diameter
Lampworked; transparent soda-lime and dichroic glass; silver foil
Photo by Jack Dewitt

Center right: Susan Breen Silvy
Fleur-de-lis, 2002
3.2 x 2.5 x 1.3 cm
Sculpted reduction; soda-lime glass; fine silver overlay
Photo by Jeff O'Dell

Bottom: Pam Hogarth, *Pixie Dust Mix*, 2004
1 x 2 x 2 cm (large); 1.2 x 1.1 x 0.4 cm (small)
Lampworked; transparent soda-lime glass; pixie dust
Photo by artist

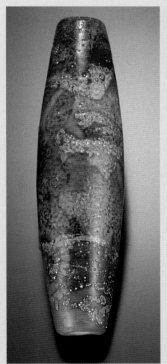

Top: Inara Knight, *Garden of My Mind*, 2002
5.7 x 3.8 x 0.9 cm (largest)
Lampworked; soda-lime glass; tabular, frit, and dichroic
inclusions; surface trailing
Photo by Jeff O'Dell

Bottom left: Sara Hoyt, *Glow*, 2004
5.2 x 1.5 x 1.5 cm
Lampworked; soda-lime glass; silver leaf, reduction frit,
and transparent layered dots
Photo by artist

Bottom center: Alethia Donathan, *Riverrock,* 2003
5 x 0.6 cm
Lampworked; soda-lime glass; enamel, copper, silver,
and reduction frits
Photo by Azad

Bottom right: Inara Knight, *Textures*, 2002
6.4 x 3.8 x 0.6 cm
Lampworked; soda-lime glass; tabular, frit, dichroic, and goldleaf
inclusions; surface trailing and copper electroformed patina
Photo by Jeff O'Dell

113

Top left: Louise Mehaffey
Silver Lining, 2003
4.4 x 3.5 x 1.3 cm
Lampworked; soda-lime glass; silver foil
Photo by Jerry Anthony

Top right: Martha Giberson
Glass Jewels, 2001
61 x 3.8 cm
Lampworked; soda-lime glass; palladium leaf
Photo by Steve Gyurina

Center: Debby Weaver
Three Silver Core Beads, 2001
2.5 x 2.5 cm to 2.5 x 3.75 cm
Lampworked; soft Italian glass; silver leaf
wrapped core encased with transparent glass,
reduction frit, and fine silver wire
Photo by artist

Bottom: Sher Berman
Extreme Enamels, 2003
3.2 x 2.5 cm (largest)
Lampworked; soda-lime glass; enamel
Photo by Greg Kuepfer

Top left: Linda MacMillan, *Pathways,* 2003
2.5 x 3.8 x 0.3 cm each
Lampworked; soda-lime and dichroic glass; black core
Photo by Robert Diamante

Bottom left: Norma Shapiro, *Collection of Dichroic
Patchwork Quilt Tube Beads,* 2003
1.9 x 3.2 x 1.9 cm each
Lampworked; dichroic and soda-lime glass; patches
applied separately onto base tube
Photo by artist

Top right: Aline Peterson, *Naked Peacock with Goosebumps,* 2003
2 x 3.5 x 2 cm
Lampworked; soda-lime glass; dichroic overlay with clear dots and precious metals
Photo by Dina A. Rossi

Center right: Kim Manchester, *Two Beads,* 1999
1.3 x 1.9 cm (left); 1.9 x 3.8 cm (right)
Layered dichroic glass; dichroic stringer embellishments
Photo by artist

Bottom right: Alethia Donathan, *Hawaiian Lava Series,* 1999
1.9 cm diameter each
Lampworked; soda-lime glass; silver
Photo by Azad

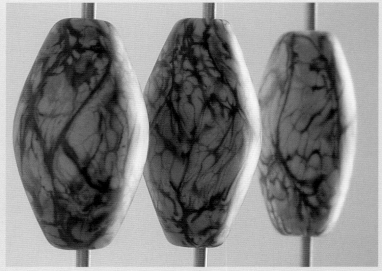
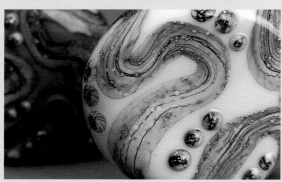

Top left: Nancy Driver
Cataract Canyon, 2003
3.3 x 2.8 x 1.0 cm
Soda-lime glass core and glass shards; silver leaf and goldstone stringer
Photo by Roger Davis

Top right: Travis Medak
Lapidary Beads, 2003
3.2 x 1.9 cm each
Lampworked; soda-lime glass; tumbled
Photo by artist

Center left: Laura Bowker
Pathways, 2003
3 x 2.5 x 1.2 cm to 2.5 x 3 x 1.2 cm
Lampworked; soda-lime glass; silver foil
Photo by Roger Schreiber

Center middle: Amy Waldman
Marble Ivory Lace, 2003
4.5 x 1.6 x 1.6 cm
Lampworked; soda-lime glass and fine silver
Photo by artist

Center right: Lisa Walsh
Ivory and Silver Bicone, 2000
3.8 x 1.9 x 1.9 cm
Flamewound; soft Italian glass; silver leaf
Photo by Richard Reid

Bottom: Michael Mangiafico
Claw, 2003
5 x 3 x 0.5 cm
Lampworked; soda-lime glass; baking soda
Photo by Joelle Levitt

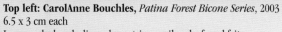

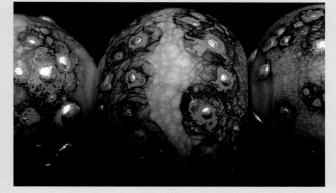

Top left: CarolAnne Bouchles, *Patina Forest Bicone Series*, 2003
6.5 x 3 cm each
Lampworked; soda-lime glass; stringer, silver leaf, and frit
Photo by Robert Diamante

Bottom left: Kristina Logan, *Three Ivory Totem Beads*, 2003
7.3 x 1.9 x 1.9 cm each
Lampworked; soda-lime glass; applied stringers
Photo by Paul Avis

Top right: Cynthia Saari, *Squares*, 2003
4.4 x 1.6 x 0.95 cm
Lampworked and wound; soda-lime glass; copper and silver foil
Photo by Ralph Gabriner

Center right: Jason Morrissey, *Silver-Fused Beads,* 2002
2.5 x 3.2 cm each
Lampworked in reducing flame; soda-lime glass and fine silver
Photo by Robert Diamante

Bottom right: Nancy Driver, *Deep Water*, 2003
3 x 1.8 x 1.8 cm
Soda-lime glass core and glass shards; silver leaf and stringer
Photo by Roger Davis

The techniques covered in this final chapter of the book will take you to a new and exciting level of beadmaking. If you've worked your way up to this point in the book, you'll have a substantial technical vocabulary as well as a good understanding of how glass behaves when heated.

The chapter is divided into four sections. First, you'll learn about fuming with metals, which adds a special glow to the surface of a bead. Next, the sections on hollow beads and sculpture introduce you to making larger beads and representational shapes, utilizing your understanding of how glass moves. The section on sculptural beads is authored and demonstrated by Kate Fowle Meleney, whose beautiful work is widely known.

The third section, which describes making your own canes, both latticino and millefiore, will give you unlimited possibilities for decorating your beads with complex ornamentation to make your beads uniquely your own. The final section covers floral beads, an incredibly popular beadmaking technique. It's no wonder, since the results are stunning! Immerse yourself in trying out this means of embellishing beads under the guidance of the accomplished Deanna Griffin Dove, who authored this section of the book.

Fuming

Fuming involves transferring gold or silver to a bead from a rod that has been charged with the metal. This process adds luster and sheen to the bead's surface. Metal particles are pushed from the rod through the air by the heat and flame's force, depositing a very thin metal coating on the warm bead.

Gold leaf and fine silver bezel are two metals that can be used for fuming. (You can also use gold wire for fuming, but the wire must be 24 karat.) The gold leaf creates a pink metallic look and silver bezel creates an earth-tone (sometimes yellow-amber) metallic or iridized effect. We'll explore these metals in the following section

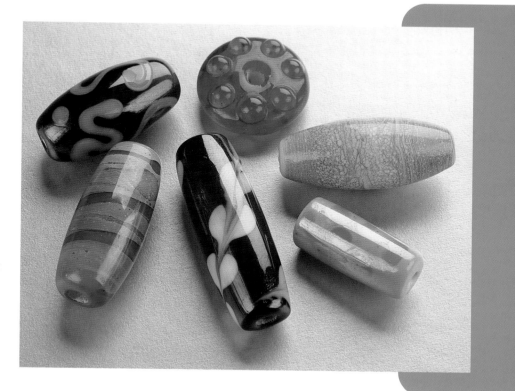

Charging the Rod

To transfer the metal to the fuming rod, you'll be working in a very hot part of the flame. For this reason, use borosilicate or quartz glass rod as a charging rod. These types of glass take longer to heat and turn molten than soft glass.

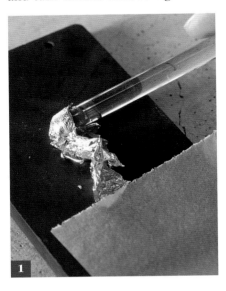

NOTE

Make sure to take safety precautions when fuming. Due to the size of the metal particles released, ordinary dust masks won't protect you from inhaling them. Therefore, it's extremely important to have good ventilation that pulls fumes away from you as well as out of your studio. If you have a visitor in your studio while you're working, make sure they stand behind you, away from the torch.

The purity of the metal that you choose also influences the safety of fuming. Purchasing pure gold leaf (24-karat gold) and fine silver will help you avoid less pure versions that can contain other, potentially dangerous metals.

Use a short piece of rod, about 6 inches (15.2 cm) long and 8 to 10 mm thick. (A thinner rod will heat and soften too quickly.) Heat the end of the rod until it is a dull orange or almost molten.

To apply gold leaf to the rod, roll it on a whole sheet of leaf so that it folds and overlaps on the hot portion (photo 1). Briefly bring the rod back into the flame to fuse the gold well (photo 2). Place this rod to the side while you're making a bead.

To apply silver, cut off a 6-inch (15 cm) piece of fine silver bezel or a longer piece of fine silver wire. Hold the square-off (nipped) end of the borosilicate rod or quartz glass rod slightly below the flame in one hand, and use the other hand to pick up the silver. Bring the rod and fine silver together just below and to the side of the flame, and move them slowly toward the flame until the silver melts and balls up. Allow the molten silver to flow onto the top of the rod. Move away from the flame, keeping the rod upright (photo 3). Allow the silver and the glass to cool and harden.

Fuming a Bead

Fuming a bead demands very careful timing. If the bead is too hot when you fume it, the metals will burn off; if the bead is too cool, the metal can flake or rub off later.

Begin by warming the bead to a medium orange glow and take it out of the flame. Slightly reduce

the amount of oxygen so that the cones at the tip of the flame grow softer and bushier. Start counting in seconds. When you reach 12, put the prepared fuming rod into the side of the flame close to the end of the cones.

Heat the fuming rod while continuing to count. At 15 seconds, bring the bead into the flame about 12 inches (30.5 cm) from the fuming rod. As the metal heats up, the fuming rod will emit a bright flare with a green tinge. Place the bead in the path of this flare to pick up the gold or silver particles (photo 4). The longer you hold the bead in the flare, the more metal accumulates. Check your progress as you work, and stop when the desired amount of metal is deposited.

As previously mentioned, the silver deposit will look yellowed and earthy, especially on ivory (as shown on the bead pictured to the left.). If you now change the flame back to a neutral one (since the balance of the flame was changed during fuming), you can heat the bead more to create different surface colors (as shown on the other bead pictured here). For instance, if you heat an ivory bead that has been fumed, the yellow becomes etched with dark lines, while the other colors will look cloudy, blue, or green (depending on the base bead color). If you're fuming with gold, too much heat will burn it off.

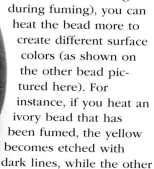

Hollow Beads

Making hollow beads allows you to make larger but lightweight beads. The following section explores several ways to make these fascinating beads. These beads can be filled with smaller beads or with trinkets and other materials. You can also decorate the outside of these beautiful forms.

Wrapped Hollow Beads

To make a hollow bead, you can begin by making two small discs about 5/8 inch (1.6 cm) apart on a regular-sized mandrel (photo 1). The distance between these two points will determine the bead's length. Beginning relatively small will allow you to work your way up as your skill increases. Wrap the small end beads carefully so they're perpendicular to the mandrel. (If you don't wrap these well, you won't be able to create good indentations later on in the process.)

Continue to wrap molten glass around one of the discs and build it up (photo 2, next page). Then move to the other disc and build that one up in the same way, shifting the wraps toward one another to create two bowl shapes (photo 3, next page).

Keep switching back and forth as you build the glass, keeping both sides warm in the flame by bathing them lightly with heat. If you don't, one side will get chilled while you're working on the other. You can seal the center between the shapes in a couple of ways: wrap the glass until both sides touch or use a graphite paddle to gently push the sides closer together.

You can also make a hollow bead by building it primarily in one direction. Try this if you're having trouble wrapping the bead evenly. Move from one side to the other,

building a bead more akin to a bowl with a lid (photo 4).

After you bring the sides together on either of these types of beads, check for holes in the wrapping. Even the smallest separation will allow air to escape, and the bead will collapse. If a hole is detected, seal it up with a dot of molten glass.

After the bead is sealed, heat the whole bead by turning it in a

flame directed at the center of the bead, so that the glass begins to smooth out (photo 5). Heat the whole bead evenly, because if one spot is overheated, the area can open up, causing the bead to collapse. As the bead heats and becomes molten, it will shrink slightly. Then the bead will expand due to the trapped hot air, and the glass will smooth out in response.

At this point, you can carefully shape and decorate the bead. Do this gently to prevent breaking the bead loose from its mandrel. Make sure the bead has cooled off enough to be fairly rigid when you decorate it.

Use very gentle heat to coax indentations into each end of a hollow bead. Because the wall of glass is thin compared to a solid bead, the indentation will end up being smaller.

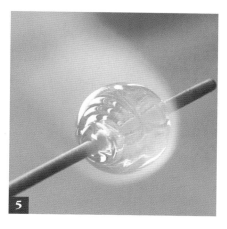

Variations

This section explores some common variations on making a wrapped hollow bead or form. As you explore hollow beads, you may even discover your own!

First, you can wrap a small bead between the end discs before covering it with a hollow bead (photo 6). When you coil the glass, avoid making contact with the interior bead. As you do this, it's very important to keep the inner bead warm but not molten. To keep it warm, you might need to slightly alter the angle at which you wrap the bead. Finish the hollow bead as described in the previous section, heating it carefully and evenly (photo 7).

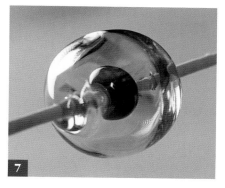

As another variation, you can create a hollow vessel with a solid bottom. To do this, wind one end of the bead so that it's right at the end of the mandrel, which will help support the hollow form as it's being made (photo 8). Transparent glass is a nice choice for this kind of form.

After mastering the previous technique, you can also begin a hollow form near the end of the mandrel, allowing you to wrap it completely off the end (photo 9). While this is much more difficult to do, the free end of the form will be completely transparent without a hole from the mandrel (a balloon-shape of sorts).

When wrapping this form, separate the glass rod often, and flash the attached end of the form in the flame. Remember to keep the whole bead relatively warm without getting it so hot that it collapses. Learning to work with just the right amount of heat takes time to understand. The vessel always has the potential of collapsing until it's been completely sealed at the bottom. Gently use a graphite paddle, marver, and gravity to shape the glass.

As another variation, consider using larger mandrels or thin-walled steel tubing to make hollow beads or forms. Both contain more surface area for holding the bead in place while it's being made. They are also easier to hold in your hand.

If you wrap a hollow form off the end of a larger mandrel, the mouth of it will be wider, allowing you to fill it with small materials such as shredded paper, tiny beads, or trinkets.

If you wrap a hollow form off the end of thin-walled steel tubing, keep in mind that air escapes through the tube. Thus, if the bubble begins collapsing, puff lightly through the end of the tubing to inflate the form. Use a gentle breath until you're accustomed to how the glass expands. Rotate the mandrel (tubing) while you blow.

Cleaning Hollow Beads and Forms

Cleaning hollow beads takes patience. After the mandrel is removed, you can use a bead reamer to break up and remove some of the trapped release. You can break up the rest of it with a long, thin sewing needle. On hollow forms with only one open end, the needle is especially handy. You can also use a tiny squeeze bottle or a medicine syringe to shoot water into the form and then draw out the water and residue.

Sculptural Techniques

KATE FOWLE MELENEY

One of the wonderful things about glass is how easily it lends itself to sculpting. It is a graceful and additive process that is both fun and challenging. Working with the glass in this capacity will teach you even more about how it responds to heat and gravity, how it is shaped, and what happens when you add glass to glass. Learning to create a certain shape and retain it will take some practice.

Simple bead shapes that you've worked with—such as spherical, tabular, and cylindrical—are all fairly consistent or even in volume. With practice, they aren't too difficult to keep evenly heated. However, manipulating glass to make sculptural beads requires more skill in this area.

In this section you'll see three sculptural/figurative beads made in sequential steps, teaching you basic principles as you go along. And, of course, there is no teacher like experience, particularly with this kind of work. But first, here are a few practical tips that will make things a bit easier before you begin:

 Begin by thinking about the shape of the bead you want to create. Draw a sketch and then search for spheres, cones, bi-cones, or cylinders as the base shapes of your form. Using common shapes is the key to this work, and it will make the beadmaking process easier to repeat later if you decide to make multiples of a bead. For instance, the winged heart described in this section is based on a cone-shaped bead, and the seashell's foundation is a small cylinder with a cone added to one end.

 When making sculptural beads, use as many premade or precut parts as possible. For instance, the heart incorporates two equal-sized pieces of rod cut ahead of time for the lobes, allowing you to make the heart symmetrical. Be sure to warm these parts in advance on a torch-top marver or hot plate to prevent thermal shock when they're applied.

 Keep in mind that you'll be building the form from the mandrel out. For this reason, it's helpful to keep notes when making a new bead, since the first try probably won't be perfect. You'll find the best order for doing things, and details that you might have assumed you'd add at the end, might come closer to the beginning of the process.

 You can manipulate the glass with glass rods and stringers as well as tools. A rod of glass or stringer can be used as a tool to pull away extra glass as long as the unwanted glass is hot and the glass tool is cool. This technique is illustrated on the wing of the heart, since a bit of extra glass is pulled away with a narrow rod, giving the wing's end a delicate point.

 You'll have to adjust your torch flame to different sizes during the sculptural process. In this case, it's okay to reduce the size of the flame by turning down the propane. However, you shouldn't use this flame for extended periods of time. But you can use it to remove tool marks from a section of the bead without melting or distorting other details. Since the rest of the bead will cool off while you're working

125

on a small detail or a trouble spot, return to the normal mix after a short period of time and bathe the entire bead in heat.

♦ Maintaining adequate heat in the bead is important while you're working on a sculptural bead. Keep the smallest parts of the bead warm, since these parts tend to cool off first. Bring such areas to a dull orange glow from time to time to make sure that it doesn't thermal shock. For example, the base of the Aegean urn that you'll see demonstrated later must be repeatedly bathed in heat while you're working on handles on the opposite end.

♦ When concentrating on a technically difficult application of glass (such as a lip, wrap, or handles), don't forget to pay attention to the portion of the bead that's been out of the heat while you do this. (For example, when you finish adding a the lip to the top of the Aegean urn [see page 131], you'll immediately go to the other end to warm it up before you finish shaping the lip.)

♦ In general, work from the base bead and add larger parts. Shape the bead as needed. Add indentions next, since they are less vulnerable to heat. After that, add the finer details last. Work around the bead so that you are able to keep the whole thing warm.

♦ Any appendages, such as arms, handles, flower petals, or wings, are particularly vulnerable to both breaking and thermal shocking. These problems can occur as the bead is being made as well as at the cooling stage. Therefore, a bead with these design elements should be put directly into a kiln for annealing.

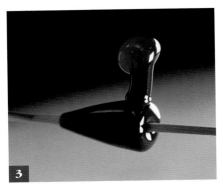

Winged Heart

Making a winged heart will introduce you to several sculptural processes. In essence, it involves adding precut pieces to a cone shape to form the upper lobes of the heart. You'll learn how to concentrate the heat on certain areas to shape them. Then you'll add "wings" or "fins" to the heart.

To begin, choose a color for your bead and have several rods on hand. Begin by nipping two 1½ inch (3.8 cm) pieces of this color rod with tile nippers. Preheat them on a torch-top marver or hot plate.

Build a cone on your mandrel and shape it well (photo 1). (The cone pictured is about 1 inch [2.5 cm] long.) Use pliers to pick up one of the cut-glass rod pieces, and preheat it in the cooler part of the

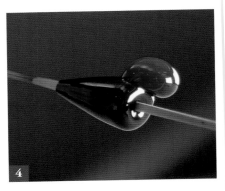

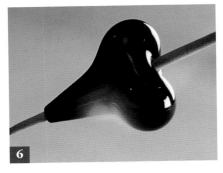

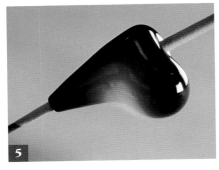

flame. When it's nicely warmed, concentrate the flame on it, and heat it until it begins to melt and glows orange. Place it at the top of the cone, and push it into the bead as shown (photo 2, previous page). This piece will be formed into the first lobe of the heart.

Once the rod is firmly in place, concentrate the flame on the top of the rod so that it melts down onto itself (photo 3, previous page). Hold the mandrel so that the molten glass doesn't flop over sideways onto the cone. Allow it to melt down into a rounded shape that droops over the cone's top edge (photo 4, previous page).

Turn down the propane to create a concentrated flame. Aim it at the lobe piece where it joins the cone. Use heat to soften this sharp area so that it smoothes out and is tapered (photo 5, previous page). Next, concentrate the heat on the bulk of the lobe, using the pull of gravity and the angle of the mandrel to encour-

age a graceful shape. Learning to do this will take some practice, but it's fun. Watch out for a couple of things: don't let the bottom of the heart cool off too much as you work on the lobe and don't allow the lobe to flop over onto the mandrel. Repeat this process for the second lobe (photo 6, previous page).

After you've finished shaping the heart, you can decorate it, if you wish. Press the designs in with the help of a graphite paddle and don't overheat the bead or you might lose its shape. Use the edge of your paddle or a knife to reach difficult areas.

To create a cleavage line at the top of the heart, aim a concentrated pinpoint flame between the two lobes where the mandrel emerges. Take the bead out of the flame, and press a palette knife or other sharp edge into the bead parallel to the mandrel (photo 7). Repeat this on the other side of the heart.

Next you'll add wings to the bead. Here we'll introduce you to two variations, one shown on one side of the heart and one on the other. However, you'll probably want to create matching wings, so choose one variation.

For the first variation, choose a rod in a color of your choice. (We used a contrasting transparent color.) Begin by developing a large ball of glass on the end of it. Lightly touch down the glass right below the lobe, and pull it along the side of the bead to lobe's top edge. Pull the glass away from the bead slightly and flame-cut it (photo 8). Heat another ball of glass and repeat this stroke on the other side to create a matching wing. Adjust the size or placement of the wings on either side by adding a small amount of glass or pulling a little away to make them even.

Heat one of the wings to an orange glow and use the pliers to flatten it several times along its length (photo 9). Don't pinch too close to the heart of the lobe, or you'll distort it. Gently heat the wing to remove any tool marks. Make several indentations along the length of each wing by heating it up about every 1/4 inch (6 mm) and pushing in the glass with your knife (photo 10). Repeat this process on the opposite wing.

To put a finishing touch on the wings, pull a little glass off the top of each to give them a visual lift. Heat the tip of the wing, and use a rod of the same color to swipe the top edge, pulling away a bit of glass. Carefully flame-cut the

7

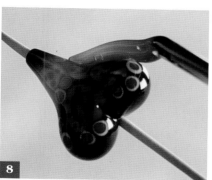

8

9

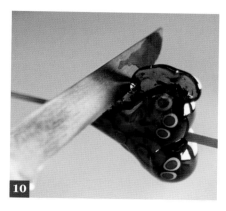

10

connecting threads (photo 11). If you're careful with the heat, the tips of the wings won't retract much and will be nicely uplifted.

To create a less frilly wing, develop a healthy ball of molten glass at the end of a rod. Touch the glass down at the bottom of the lobe and pull it up to the top of the lobe (photo 12). Pull away a small amount of glass to create the wing tip before flame-cutting it (photo 13). Allow this ridge of glass to cool slightly while you heat a second ball of glass.

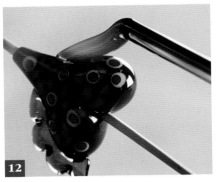

Add more glass on top of this ridge, beginning the stroke slightly higher on top of the previous one (photo 14). End the second stroke at the tip of the first one. As described for the previous wing, heat the tip and pull away a bit of glass before flame-cutting it to give the wing a feeling of motion (photos 15 and 16). Repeat this process on the other side of the bead. As usual, anneal the bead in the kiln after you're done.

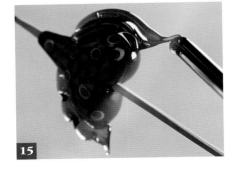

Spiral Seashell

The following bead is based on the Junonia shell. Even though it looks complex, it is also built from a simple base shape—in this case, a tubular core with a cone shape added over one end. You'll carefully build the opening flap of the shell and then decorate the entire shape with a twist. Making this form will teach you how to carefully place the heat to retain the shape while enhancing it.

For this bead you'll need a few pre-made components, including several twisted stringers that combine ivory and dark amber (sometimes called topaz) and a stringer of pale or opalino pink.

Use the smallest mandrel available, .045 inch (0.11 cm) in diameter, so that the core is delicate and doesn't overpower the rest of the bead. Coat the mandrel with release past the center, leaving one end free so that you can flip the bead back and forth as you work.

Begin by laying down a small tubular-shaped core of ivory glass that is about 1¹⁄₃ inches (3.4 cm) long. Smooth out the core with a paddle (photo 1, next page). Build a ⁵⁄₈-inch (1.6 cm) long cone on the left side of the core, placing the narrow end at the tube's end and building towards the center of it (photo 2, next page). Use a graphite paddle to make the cone smooth and symmetrical.

To build the shell's flap, attach a small ball of ivory glass to the wide edge of the cone at the bottom. It should fill the 90° angle formed by the core tube and the end of the cone (photo 3). Pull the glass away slightly and wrap it along the length of the core, rotating the bead a quarter turn away from you to distribute the glass. Taper the glass and flame-cut it at the end of the tube (photo 4).

Allow the glass to cool slightly while you heat another small ball of glass to molten. Touch down the molten glass on top of the previously wrapped glass and draw it along the edge, turning the bead toward you as needed. Taper the glass to a small point and flame-cut it. Continue to lay down wraps in the same manner to build the lip of the opening. Add around seven more wraps, turning the bead toward you with each stroke (photo 5).

After building the base shape, add the twisted ivory and amber stringer for decoration. Heat the twist so that it softens and you can attach the end of it to the small end of the cone. Wrap the twist so that it spirals around the cone until it overlaps the flap (photo 6). Carefully flame-cut it at the edge of the flap.

Continue applying the twist to the bottom edge of the cone, connecting it under the flap and wrapping it around to the outer side of the flap (photo 7). End the twist at the lip of the flap, and flame-cut it. Continue covering the shell with wraps of the twist, beginning on the core tube underneath the flap

and wrapping around the top (photo 8). Flame-cut the stringer each time you add a wrap.

After you've covered the flap, melt in the twists, beginning at the end of the cone. Gently heat the twists and press them with the narrow side of a graphite paddle to smooth the cane on the cone.

Once the twist is melted into the cone, turn your attention to the flap of the shell. Turn down the propane on your flame to make it a

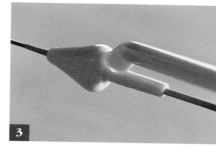

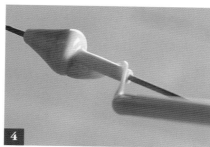

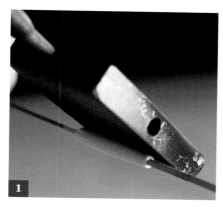

By using a graphite paddle, you can minimize the amount of heat necessary to melt the cane flush because the graphite doesn't chill the glass like a metal tool does. The use of less heat (and reheating) helps maintain the base shell shape you've established.

9

10

pinpoint size, allowing you to get into tight places without melting the whole bead (photo 9). Gently heat it, and then use flat-nose pliers to press the twist into the flap until it is smoothed (photo 10).

When you're heating the area that's near the right end (end of the flap), be careful not to heat the opening until it's misshapen. Remember, you can work with this kind of flame for only a short period of time before returning to

11

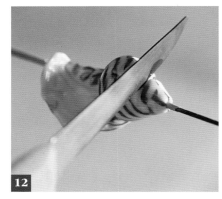

12

13

a neutral one. Use this kind of flame as you press the twist inside the bead's flap near its delicate right opening (photo 11).

Next, you'll accentuate the spiral by creasing a spiraling line around the shell with a paring knife (photo 12). To do this, flip the bead and hold the other end of the mandrel so that you can reach the cone end more easily. The knife should be cool so that it doesn't stick to the glass. Preheat the cone, and then press with the knife to make a crease that runs from the beginning of the flap on the cone to the narrow point. Obviously, you'll need to turn the

14

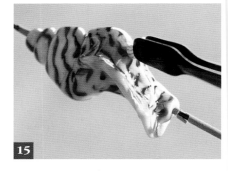

15

16

bead as you do this. You might have to do this in two steps if the bead begins to cool off and needs to be reheated.

To add a pink blush to the inside of the shell, apply the opalino or pale pink stringer to the lip of the flap (photo 13, previous page). Heat the flap gently and use pliers to push in the stringer. Pinch the flap of the shell, leaving it with a pretty ruffle (photo 14, previous page). You can add a finishing touch that resembles barnacles by applying slices of cane to the shell (photo 15, previous page).

When you're finished, anneal the bead in the kiln. Annealing will prevent cracking that can easily happen because of the differing thicknesses of the cone and the flap (photo 16, previous page).

After annealing, you can etch the outside of the shell in acid to give it a matte finish, if you wish. To protect the delicate pink interior and serve as a resist to the acid, paint it with nail polish. After dipping it in acid, remove the polish with acetone remover.

Aegean Urn

This bead emulates an ancient vessel that has been pulled from the sea by archeologists. The etched surface mimics the effects created by the ocean over the years, and it is also decorated with gold leaf and enamels. Small barnacle canes can also be added to its surface.

When you make a vessel bead, it's very important to maintain a balance of heat between the larger and smaller parts of the piece so that it doesn't thermal shock. You'll be dealing with various volumes of glass. For instance, the large body of the vessel holds heat much longer than the delicate neck and handles. Think ahead about this when planning the steps for making any kind of vessel. Decorate as much of the body of the piece as you can before adding the neck and handles, and you'll have a better chance of producing a vessel without cracks.

For the conical bottom section of the vessel, lay down a core about 2½ inches (6.4 cm) long. The end that will serve as the vessel's bottom should have a neat dimpled opening. Then add glass to this core to create a cone shape as you did in the shell project described previously. Make sure that the cone is centered around the mandrel.

To expedite this process, make this cone by applying a larger amount of glass more quickly with a wider diameter (13 to 14 mm) glass rod (photo 1). If you have smaller rods, you can bundle three rods together with a rubber band and use it to apply the glass.

After you've wrapped the glass, smooth and shape it with a graphite paddle. Use a palette knife to make indentations around the length of the cone, parallel with the mandrel (photo 2). Apply gold leaf to the warm bead (photo 3), and use the palette knife to smooth it out (photo 4).

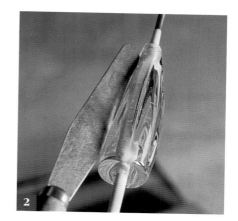

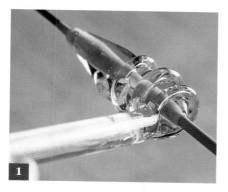

To create the neck of the vessel, make a small round bead at the end of the cone situated as close to it as possible without touching it. Make sure the bead is centered before giving it a bit of heat and using the side of a graphite paddle to flatten it out and increase its length in both directions (photo 5). As it gets longer, it will meet the cone and attach itself to it. Follow up with a pinpoint flame at the angle where the neck meets the cone to make certain they're completely fused (photo 6).

Before adding the vessel's lip, bathe the entire bead with heat to make sure that the bottom doesn't cool off too much. Then form a slightly firm medium-sized ball of glass and delicately attach it to the top edge of the neck. Wrap the molten glass around the neck one or two times, building it up like you would a very thin disc bead. You can wrap more glass if you want the lip to be more extended. When you're finished,

taper off and flame-cut the rod as you complete the final rotation (photo 7). Slowly heat away the seam lines of the lip with short doses of heat. Use a graphite paddle to align the glass as needed. Don't forget to keep the rest of the bead warm while you work on this!

To make the handles, you can use either a stringer or rod of glass. Begin by placing a dot of glass on the vessel's lip where you want the handle to connect. Place another dot in the same latitude, indicating the bottom of the handle. In this case, this dot is on the upper part of the cone. Heat the dots in well without flattening them totally. To mark a point of reference for the halfway point on your urn, put a small dot of glass on the mandrel just past the lip of the bead and on the same latitude (photo 8).

5

6

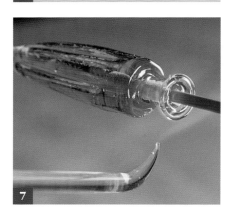

7

8

9

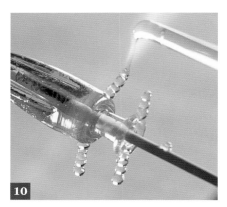

10

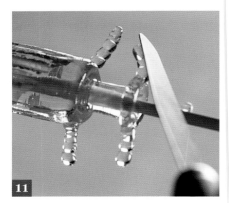

11

12

Turn the bead around halfway and repeat the last step, placing dots in the same place on the opposite side of the bead (photo 9, previous page). Add glass on top of each of these four dots, and allow the added molten glass to cool slightly before adding another dot. Build up small pillars of glass with the dots. The pictured pillars are about ¼ inch (6 mm) high (photo 10).

Heat one of the top pillars in the flame and use a knife to gently bend it towards the lower pillar on the same side (photo 11). Heat and bend the lower pillar toward the upper pillar using the same technique. If the two pairs don't touch, add a dot of glass to form a bridge. Repeat this on the other side of the vessel.

Now you've created two bumpy-looking handles. Point one handle up and apply gentle heat to it, watching it closely so that it doesn't melt onto the neck. Turn the handle down from time to time to let gravity help you (photo 12). As the glass heats to molten it will retract and the seam lines will melt into each other. Gently heat the handle and use a tungsten pick to shape it as you wish. Warm the base of the vessel again, and heat and shape the handle on the other side.

As a finishing touch, you can attach slices of cane to resemble barnacles to the vessel. Dust the vessel with enamel to give it a nice finish. Anneal the bead, as usual. Then, if you wish to give it a matte look, you can etch it in acid, which doesn't affect the gold.

Handle Variations

In this section, we cover a couple of alternative ways to make handles on a vessel. In the demonstrations that follow, one variation is shown on one side and one on the other. You might actually choose this kind of design on purpose, but, more likely, you'll match the handles!

For the first variation, begin by placing a large dot of molten glass on one side of the bead (photo 1). Heat the glass and allow it to settle onto the bead a bit (photo 2). Repeat this process on the other side of the bead, making sure that the dots are of equal volume.

Heat one of the dots to molten and mash it with a parallel press or flat-nosed pliers to make a tabular shape (photos 3 and 4). Repeat on the other side.

Warm the handle to an orange glow while also heating the end of a straight tungsten pick. To do this, alternate the handle and pick in the flame without putting them both in at the same time, preventing the pick from fuming on the glass, leaving an undesirable stain.

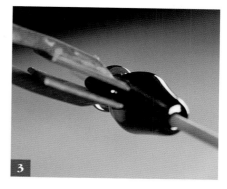

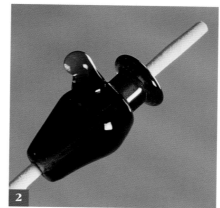

When the handle is quite soft, gently push the pick into the tab until it makes an indentation, being careful not to loosen the bead from the mandrel (photo 5). Reheat both the handle and pick and push into the handle from the opposite side. You might have to reheat the handle and pick several times before you can push all the way through to create a clean hole. Once a hole has been opened in the handle tab, it can be reheated and opened more using the pick to stretch it out and shape it as desired (photo 6). Repeat these steps on the other handle, warming up the entire bead before beginning to prevent thermal shock.

The second handle variation has a nice fluid look to it. Begin by laying down a set of four small dots (two on each side of the vessel), to mark the placement of the handles. Heat a large ball of glass to molten and place it on the side of the bead where the top of the handle goes (photo 7). Heat and place a second ball of glass on the other side, being careful to make them the same size.

Concentrate the flame on one of the handles, heating it to an orange glow. Use a pair of tweezers to pinch a bit of the molten glass and pull it away from the bead to stretch out the glass (photo 8). Pull the glass down and attach it to the bead. Release the small tab and push it into the bead (photo 9). Gently concentrate the flame on the bottom of the handle to ensure that it is fused well on the bead.

For shaping all of these handles, use gentle heat to warm the handle and a gentle hand with a pick or tweezers for shaping (photo 10). If part of the handle becomes very thin, try to keep heat away from that area, as more heat will just make it thinner.

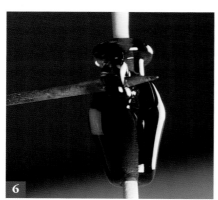

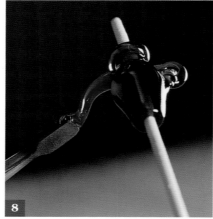

Making Decorative Canes

Making canes is one of the most fascinating ventures you'll undertake in the world of glass beadmaking. Decorative canes such as *millefiori*, *latticino*, and *murrini* are created solely for the purpose of embellishing a bead's surface. Latticino is a twisted ribbon cane that can range from simple to quite elaborate. It's applied to the outside of the bead.

Millefiori (mosaic glass) was initially developed in ancient times. The Venetians took this art to new heights of complexity during medieval times. Created by bundling together rods or smaller canes to create a cross-section pattern, these canes or murrini are sliced into small pieces that repeat the pattern.

Techniques for making these canes vary greatly, yielding more or less detail in relationship to the amount of labor involved. In this section, you'll learn to build latticino, millefiore, and murrini directly at the torch. It's possible to get great image detail and shading.

You'll begin by making some simple ribbon cane and move to more complex versions of cane. This section is arranged so that you can move comfortably from working with regular-sized canes to larger ones with greater detail. These canes require a larger volume of glass that's more difficult to control at the torch. Therefore, you'll add glass handles to it to help support the glass as you work. At the end of this section, you'll learn to create a complicated portrait cane.

Simple Ribbon Cane

Simple ribbon cane, a type of latticino, has many decorative possibilities. It is a variation on the three-color twist that you made in chapter 3 (see page 69).

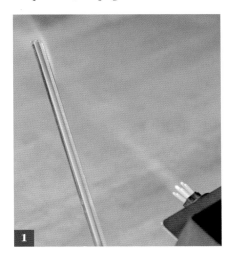

To make this type of cane, you'll need a couple of rods of filigrana (rods with cores of opaque color encased with clear glass) and a contrasting opaque or dark transparent color rod. All rods should be about the same diameter. The contrasting rod will be sandwiched between the two filigrana. Notice that we used two different colors of filigrana.

Begin by heating a filigrana rod with a glancing flame on one side only until it glows orange (photo 1). Flatten this side with a graphite paddle or on a torch-top marver. Reheat it as needed to flatten it

135

until it widens (photo 2). Place it on your rod rest, separated from other rods that might chill it. Flatten the other filigrana rod in the same way as the first, but keep this one warm in the back of the flame after you're finished.

Heat the contrasting rod to molten and paint a thin layer of it down the flattened area of the second filigrana rod (photo 3). As long as you're using a glancing flame, the filigrana should remain rigid enough for you to push the contrasting color down its length, leaving a layer of glass behind. (Notice that the rod is held at a right angle in the photo. In this demonstration, this angle indicates "painting" with the rod, a term that we'll use throughout this section.)

Heat the applied glass with a glancing flame and smooth it out with a paddle so that it meets the edge of the flattened filigrana (photo 4). Use a glancing flame along the flattened side of the other filigrana and bring it to molten. After it softens, lay it down on top of the contrasting color (photo 5). Connect the two outer filigrana rods by heating each end of the stacked area and bending the glass rod to join them (photo 6).

Heat the entire stacked area until molten. Pull and twist the cane (photo 7). You might want to leave the cane a bit thick so that the ribbon effect shows clearly in the finished cane (photo 8).

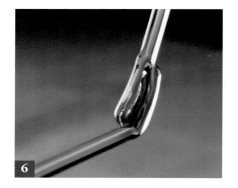

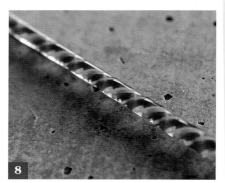

136

Encased Ribbon Cane

You can enhance a simple ribbon cane made with filigrana by completely encasing the contrasting (middle) color with clear or transparent glass, resulting in a cane with more visual depth.

Before you begin, place this clear or transparent rod within easy reach. After laying down the contrasting color and smoothing it, warm and lay down the second filigrana rod as described in the previous section. This time, however, flame-cut the second rod to leave the flattened section behind.

Bring the clear or transparent rod to molten and paint down the sides of the sandwiched area, encasing the contrasting color (photo 1). Roll the added glass on a marver to smooth it out. Heat the end of the previously cut filigrana rod and reattach it to the end of the cane. Turn the *cane mass* that you've created in the flame, rotating it and keeping it straight. Heat the whole area until it's molten and glows evenly (photo 2).

As it heats up and softens, the layered area will become football-shaped. Don't allow your hands to drift apart, and keep turning the rods back and forth to keep the glass centered. When this area is evenly melted, bring the cane mass out of the flame and pause for a few seconds. Pull and twist the cane. Notice the depth created in the finished cane (photo 3).

> **NOTE**
>
> *Since you're working with a larger volume of glass because of the added encasing, you might have trouble controlling it. If this happens, bring the piece out of the flame and let the glass cool slightly to keep it from drooping or elongating too much. When you work with even larger volumes of glass, such as the complex cane described on page 144, you'll be prepared for this challenge by practicing this maneuver now.*

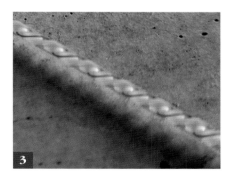

Making Handles for Canes

Before you become immersed in the following sections that explore making more complex canes, pause and read through this section on making handles and pulling the cane as a prerequisite. It explains how to work with the larger volumes of glass that you'll be using when you move on to more complex canes. You may want to refer back to this section as you are working.

Previously, you used rods of glass of the same diameter to serve as handles for holding and turning the glass in the flame. As you work with more glass, you'll need to add larger handle rods at each end of the built-up cane to serve as supports.

To make handles for the ends of the cane, you'll use soft glass along with borosilicate rods, or soft glass only. Since you're using thicker rods, they'll endure more heat and be less likely to thermal shock while the cane is being built.

Three different types of handles, described below, can be added to the ends of canes. The handles hold the mass of the cane after it's built, and assist you while you heat it in preparation for pulling it out. Before adding any sort of handle, check to see that the end of the cane mass is fairly flat, without crevices or dips that might trap air bubbles. If needed, heat and flatten the end of the cane with a graphite paddle before adding the handle.

In this section, you'll also learn how to heat the cane so that it doesn't lose its interior alignment and shape. And, you'll learn to control it as you pull it out to the desired length or thickness.

Soft Glass with Borosilicate Rod

This handle is used for pulling fairly large cane of around 2 inches (5 cm) in diameter or larger, such as picture cane (millefiore) or complex ribbon cane (latticino). Borosilicate is stiffer in the flame, so it creates a very sturdy handle. Use a clear or transparent glass rod so that you can see into the end of the cane, allowing you to judge the amount of heat in the center while checking the image as you work. When working on images, it's especially important to help avoid distorting or twisting them.

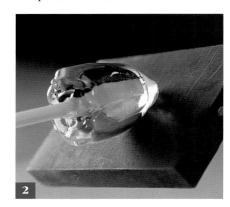

Begin by adding clear soft glass that's very molten to the end of the cane mass (photo 1), pushing it into the end to avoid trapping air bubbles. Completely cover the end to the edges. Doing this is important so that you can get an even pull that stretches all layers of the cane.

On a marver, shape the added clear glass into a cone (photo 2). Keep the cane mass warm in the

back flame, and heat a thick rod (12 to 14 mm) of clear borosilicate to molten at the torch. Shape the end to a point. Heat up both the cone and the borosilicate until they're very hot. The cane cone should be glowing orange.

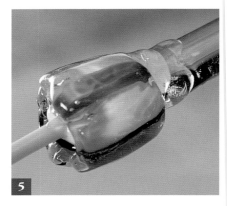

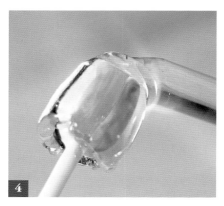

Push the rod into the cone (photo 3, previous page), and bend it to one side, thinking of this as your "north" movement (photo 4, previous page). From this point, bend it three more times to the "south," "east," "west," and back into a straight position, drawing a bit of the soft glass up onto the borosilicate rod to form a good connection (photo 5, previous page). Make sure the rod is now aligned with the center of the mass. Move to the other end of the cane where the core color rod is located.

To create a handle on the other end of the cane, heat the original handle (the thin rod of the first color used to make the cane) in the flame until molten and separate it from the cane mass (photo 6). Take a look at this end of the cane and make sure that it's fairly even with no crevices or dips that might trap bubbles. If the end is uneven, heat it in the flame and flatten it on a marver (photo 7). Build up a cone with soft glass, as you did on the other end, and attach another borosilicate rod to this end.

Soft Glass Rod

Rather than using borosilicate glass for the handles, you can use a large soft glass rod (12-14 mm) for cane masses that are about 1½ inches (3.8 cm) or less. After the cane has been pulled and the handles nipped off, you don't have to worry about incompatibility issues that might cause breakage, as you do when using borosilicate handles. When you use soft glass, you must apply less heat to the end cones as you approach the pulling stage, since the end cones have to stay cooler and firmer to remain stable.

Borosilicate Maria Handles

These particular handles made from borosilicate work well for a cane mass that is approximately 1 inch (2.5 cm) or less. They are built by creating what is called a maria at the end of two borosilicate rods. To make a *maria*, heat the end of a borosilicate rod (12 to 14 mm) until a small ball of glass forms. Hold the rod perpendicular to the marver and push the ball straight down so that the molten glass is pressed outward, creating something that looks like the head of a nail (photo 8). Set aside these rods until you need them.

After the cane has been built, add a layer of clear molten soft glass, being careful to cover the entire end of the cane mass. Flatten the glass on the end of the cane, and heat it to an orange glow. Warm up a borosilicate maria handle until it is barely glowing. Push the handle into the molten glass and rock it back and forth a bit to secure and center it on the end of the cane (photo 9). Move to the other end of the cane mass, flame-cut the original handle, and flatten the end. Coat the end with clear glass and connect the other borosilicate maria handle.

Pulling the Cane

After you've attached stable handles to each end of the cane mass, you're ready to heat it and pull it down to a smaller diameter. Turn up both the oxygen and propane to slightly increase the size of the flame, balancing the gases. Hold the cane horizontally by the handles and aim the flame directly at the cane.

Move the cane back and forth to heat the entire length of the cane mass. Rotate it and heat it all the way around (photo 10). Occasionally hold the cane at an angle so that the flame shoots into one of the ends where the handle is attached and into the center of the cane. As the outside layers of glass heat up, they'll be more difficult to control. To help with this, roll the cane on a marver, pushing heat into the center of the cane while cooling the outside and firming it up a bit.

Continue heating the cane until it is molten all the way through. To check it, bring it out of the flame and pull the handles apart slightly. If the cane pulls out only at the ends and has a football shape, the inside isn't hot enough. Instead, the entire cane mass should begin to elongate when you pull it.

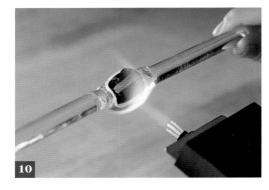

10

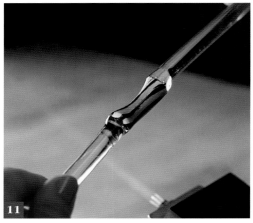

11

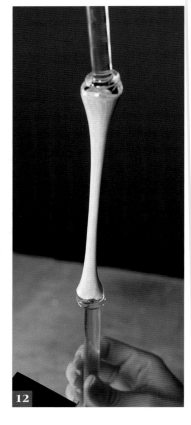

12

After you've heated the cane all the way through, bring it out of the flame and pause a few seconds to allow the outside to firm up slightly. Your goal is to pull the cane so that it has a consistent diameter all the way down its length. The center shouldn't be too thin, nor the ends too fat.

Begin pulling with the cane held almost horizontally (photo 11). If the cane starts to droop in the middle, move to a vertical position with the heaviest end on top (photo 12). Since heat rises, the thickest part of the cane will become the hottest when you hold the cane in this position. Continue to pull until the cane is the desired thickness.

After pulling the cane, lay it on the tabletop until it firms up enough to remove the handles with nippers. Cut the cane on each end at a spot where all of it has pulled out evenly.

If you've used borosilicate handles, it's especially important to do this as quickly as possible, since the glass is very incompatible and thermal shock will set in.

Now that you understand the technique of building handles and using them to pull (or draw) the cane down to a thinner size, you can approach making more complex canes that require large cane masses, including millefiore and complex latticino.

Simple Layered Millefiori

In this section you'll learn how to make the simplest versions of mille-fiore. The simple exercise that follows will show you how cane is built from the inside out. You'll need colored opaque rods for the cane mass and clear or transparent glass for the handles.

Choose a color rod to use as the center of your design, and warm it slightly in the cooler part of the flame. Select a second color to surround the central one, heat the end of this rod to molten, and use it to encase the first rod. Paint the glass down the side of the rod at a 90° right angle, or skim it down the side at approximately a 45° angle to produce a thinner layer. When you skim with a rod, use the firm part of it to push the molten glass down the length of the rod you're encasing (photo 1). The angle that you choose determines how thick your encased color is and thus influences your design. (For instance, you can skim with a rod to produce a thin line between wider sections of color on such a cane.)

After the rod is completely encased, smooth the added layer on a marv-er or with a graphite paddle (photo 2). Even out the glass by heating it with a glancing flame. (Always use this type of flame after you've added a new layer, because you need to keep the inner rod firm and easy to handle.) If you wish, you can add more layers of glass to create a more complex design. When the final layer has been smoothed out, add the handles, heat the mass to molten, and pull the cane.

The simplest cane is made by encasing a rod with glass.

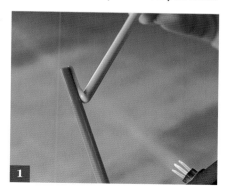

> **NOTE**
>
> *When you add a layer of glass to a millefiore cane, avoid wrapping glass over the end of the central rod or any layers you've just added. The end of the cane should always remain visible so that you can turn the rod and look at the design as you create it. Make sure that each layer you add is evenly dispersed from end to end. If needed, add a little glass to fill in at the end of the cane before rolling the glass again.*

Making Millefiori with Optic Molds

An optic mold is a metal form used to shape a molten ball of glass. This shaped glass can then be used as the central design on a cane, providing you with a nice clean image in various shapes, such as stars, moons, hearts, or flowers. After shaping the glass in a mold, you'll encase it with a layer of glass before pulling it out.

Optic milds produce clear, crisp designs.

To mold the glass, gather a large ball of glass in a color of your choice at the end of a rod. (Naturally, the volume of glass needed depends on the mold you're using.) Here, we used a large rod of clear glass (12 mm) that's easy to maneuver. As you bring the glass to molten and form a large ball, hold the rod up so that the glass flows back onto it as it heats and softens.

Next, turn the rod down and hold the ball of glass directly over the opening of the mold, allowing it to elongate slightly (photo 1). Push the molten glass down firmly into the mold. Pause for a couple of seconds and pull the glass back up and out of the mold (photo 2).

Return the molded glass back to the torch immediately to warm it up in the cooler part of the flame.

Keep the molded glass warm while you heat the encasing color to molten in the hottest portion of the flame. The molded shape should be warm enough to prevent it from cracking, but firm enough to retain its shape as you add the surrounding encasing glass. If the molded shape

has indentations, begin encasing by painting very molten glass into each furrow (photo 3). If your shape has pointed parts, such as the tips of a crescent moon, cover those first before adding glass to the rest of the shape. Your goal is to cover the whole shape with glass until you've built up a surrounding cylindrical mass that's even all the way around. You can stop with one molding and encasing, if you wish, or you can do a second molding to create a more intricate design.

To do a second molding with another optic mold of a different shape, you might need to heat the cane mass to molten and hold it vertically so that it elongates and fits into the second mold (photo 4). When you bring it out, it will retain the shape of the new mold (photo 5). Encase this form. When you've finished encasing, even up the ends, build handles, heat the cane to molten, and pull it out to the desired diameter.

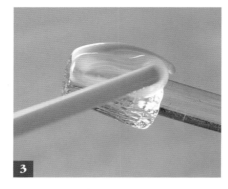

Striped Cane Made with an Optic Mold

A simple way to make a striped millefiori cane is to use a multi-pointed, star-shaped optic mold. Shape the cane mass as described in the previous section (photo 6). Then use stringers to paint stripes down the indentations that provide natural guides for placement (photos 7 and 8).

Add handles to the cane mass (photo 9). When you heat up the cane to molten, the stripes will melt into the mass (photo 10). Pull the cane, elongating the stripes (photo 11). Pull the cane down to a narrow diameter, leaving the stripes straight or twisting them slightly (photo 12).

When a slice of this cane is applied to a bead later and melted in, straight stripes will create a starburst effect while twisted cane will create a spiral pattern (see page 106 for more information).

6

7

8

9

10

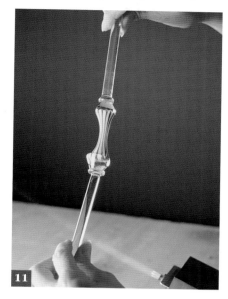

11

12

Complex Ribbon Cane

Now that you know how to deal with larger volumes of glass at the torch, you can make complex ribbon cane or latticino, which is more detailed and appears more three-dimensional when finished. Because you'll add more glass to make this cane, you'll end up with a longer length of cane.

The basis of this cane is glass formed into a paddle shape. You'll use a parallel press to do this. This paddle is then layered with colors and clear glass to create a particular pattern in the glass when it's pulled out and twisted. The design possibilities are endless, but we'll show you one version to teach you the basics. The illustration below shows this version along with three design variations.

You'll need several colored glass and clear glass rods to make this cane: one for the paddle, one for a contrasting layer, and one or two for two stripes that run down the center of each side of the paddle. Choose a contrasting color for the stripes so they'll show up well in the finished cane. Don't forget that you'll also need clear glass for the handles.

Begin by bringing a large volume of glass to molten. Hold the rod down so that the molten glass elongates slightly, then pinch it with a parallel press (photo 1). Turn the paddle so that the press can be used to square off the sides (photo 2).

To create corners, use a glancing flame to heat one edge of the paddle to bright orange. Use a warm but not molten rod of the same color to skim along the paddle edge and push the glass toward the end of it (photo 3, next page). This requires a quick movement.

You can also use a graphite paddle to square off the edges. If needed, dab molten glass on the end of the paddle near the rod to make an even, straight side. Repeat these steps for the other edge of the paddle to square the sides (photo 4, next page).

Skim or paint a layer of color on the paddle (photo 5, next page). Make sure that it is even with the paddle edges. Use a glancing flame to heat the paddle's edge to a bright molten orange and slide a rod quickly along the edge to even it up. This process will strip off a little glass. Smooth each side with a graphite paddle as needed.

Skim a thin layer of clear glass on each flat side of the paddle (photo 6, next page). Smooth this glass out with a graphite paddle (photo 7, next page).

Heat a colored rod to molten and lay a thick ridge down the center of one side of the paddle along its length to create a stripe (photo 8, next page). Make this ridge as even as possible from end to end and use tweezers to shape the ridge and keep it from sinking into the paddle (photo 9, next page). Fill in the corner along the ridge with very

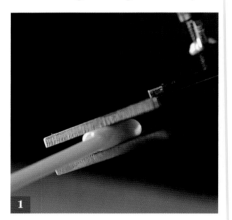

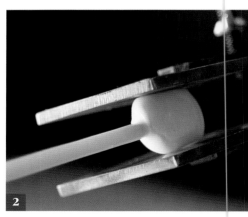

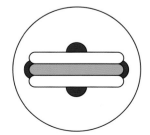

Complex ribbon cane can be varied in many ways. These are just a few of the design possibilities.

molten clear glass (photo 10). Avoid trapping air bubbles by pushing the glass at an angle. After the crevices are filled on either side of the ridge, add a layer of clear over the top to protect it (photo 11). Turn the paddle over and add a second color ridge, and cover it with a clear layer as well.

Now you're ready to encase the cane mass, working around it and painting clear glass down its length until it builds up. Encase the whole cane, including the edges of the paddles. Add clear glass until the cane is rounded off as you look at its end. Use a graphite paddle to smooth the glass in preparation for adding handles (photo 12).

Add handles as described previously and heat the cane to molten, keeping the design aligned without twisting it. When the cane is molten, pull it and twist it. This volume of glass will create a very long pull so be prepared to really stretch! You might need an assistant to help pull the cane to a size that's appropriate for application to beads, around 1/8 inch (3 mm)

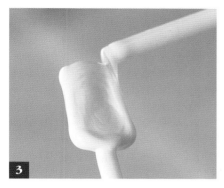

3

4

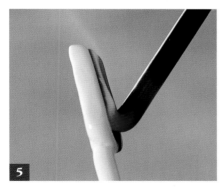

5

6

7

8

9

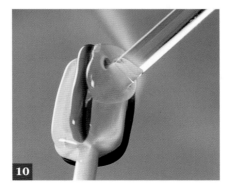

10

11

12

in diameter (photo 13). As you can see on the finished cane, the ribbon winding through the clear glass creates a dimensional effect (photo 14).

Letter and Number Canes

You can build up a stockpile of letters and numbers to have on hand when you want to add a word, your initials, or even a date to a bead (photo 1). The following section gives you two illustrated examples of block-style letters—a straight-lined T and a curved S. These two exercises will teach you basics about forming letters in cane. From there, you can guide yourself by using the illustration on page 147, which shows the most convenient order in which to build each letter and number.

Begin by choosing the colors you want to use. You'll usually use two—one for the letter and one for the background. If you want to make an entire alphabet in these two colors, have plenty of rods on hand. Use opaque colors that contrast with one another. The most obvious example is black and white, which we've used for the two exercises. Avoid opaque greens, since these colors tend to spread out to the bead's surface.

The tools that you'll need are the same as for any complex cane. They include a graphite paddle

with a knife-edge that is helpful for working with narrow angles. You'll also need a torch-top marver. If you plan to use your letters and numbers together, try to pull them to a similar diameter.

Exercise 1: Making the Letter T

To make a T, begin by making a flattened rectangular paddle of black or a dark opaque color. This paddle will end up being the upright or stem of the T. Use ivory or another light color (the background color) to build up a width of glass on each side of the paddle to support the crosspiece of the T later.

Begin this building process on one side of the paddle. Paint the first layer of glass down the side of it.

146

Smooth the layer out with a graphite paddle before adding another. Continue this process on both sides of the paddle until you build up enough glass to support the top of the T. The width of the glass on either side will determine the width of this portion of the letter.

Square off one side, perpendicular to the dark line formed by the paddle, in preparation for adding the straight crosspiece. Skim the glass with the appropriate color in areas that need smoothing (photo 2). When this area is completely flat, use the letter color to paint glass onto it, matching the thickness of the upright (photos 3 and 4).

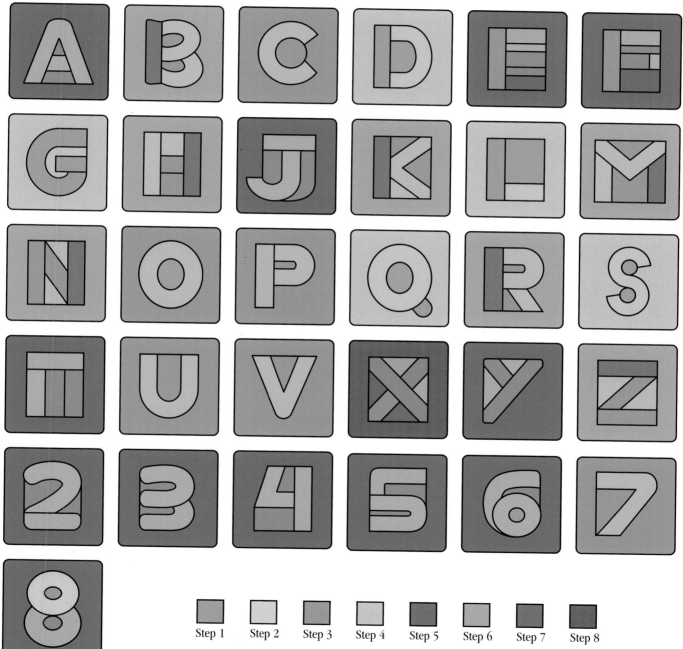

Step 1　Step 2　Step 3　Step 4　Step 5　Step 6　Step 7　Step 8

Encase the whole letter with the background color, being sure to cover the ends of the letter first to protect them (photo 5). Continue to add the background color around the sides (photo 6). Build up glass until you've created a circular piece when the cane mass is viewed from the end. If the surrounding glass is thick enough, it should protect the letter from distortion when the mass is heated (photo 7).

When the cane mass is well formed, add handles and heat the mass to molten. Roll the cane mass on a graphite marver to push heat into the center of the mass. Firm up the outer layer so that the image doesn't shift or distort. When the entire mass is evenly heated and molten (photo 8), pull the image down to a smaller size.

Exercise 2:
Making the Letter S

To make an S, begin by working with a rod of the letter color (black). Shape the end of it into a long, thin rectangular paddle and square off both ends. Warm a rod of the background color (ivory) in the end of the flame while heating the paddle to a dull orange glow. Lay the background rod across the top edge of the paddle. Roll the rod to wrap the paddle halfway around it (photo 9).

5

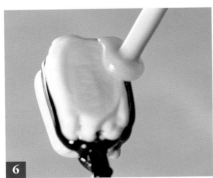

6

7

8

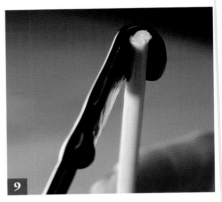

9

10

11

Flame-cut the letter color rod (black) from the paddle (photo 10, previous page). Flatten and square off the end (photo 11, previous page). Warm a second background color rod while bringing the other end of the paddle to a dull orange glow. Lay the rod across the edge of the

paddle on the opposite side. Roll this end in the opposite direction to form the other curve of the S (photo 12). Flame-cut the second background color rod at the side edge of it, leaving the other rod intact.

Use background color to fill in the curve formed by the rolled area

(photo 13). Fill in around the entire letter to form a round shape, being careful to leave the tips of the S cool enough that they don't distort while molten glass is added to them. Clean up the ends of the cane mass as needed before adding handles and pulling it to form a finished cane (photo 14).

12

13

14

Complex Picture Cane

In this section we'll explore combining smaller canes to make a larger one with a complex design. These are often called murrini. Some of the most common picture cane contains repeated representational elements such as stars, moons, or flowers. You can also use letters, numbers, or other symbols. In other words, you're creating a picture with canes, and the possibilities are as vast as painting a picture—whether representational or abstract.

Each secondary cane or visual element is created separately and then combined to make the larger cane. When you plan your design, make a sketch so that you're clear about the placement of each one. In your overall plan, divide the image into as many areas as needed.

You will usually take the preheated smaller pieces of cane out of the kiln one by one to assemble them. When you plan your design, you must figure out the orientation of each cane and place the canes in the kiln in this position. The most obvious example is a letter—if you want your T to be upright, you must place it upright in the kiln so that you can easily pick it up in the correct position.

Each secondary cane of a size larger than $3/16$ inch (5 mm) needs to be preheated in the kiln to approximately 970°F (524°C). Nip a long cane into sections about $1\frac{1}{2}$ inches (3.8 cm) long before placing them in the kiln.

Canes that are smaller than $3/16$ inch (5 mm) can be heated in the flame rather than in the kiln. Do this very

slowly, starting in the coolest part of the flame and moving up to the hotter portion.

To pick up the first and central cane out of the kiln, use a rod that is the same color as your design's background color. This rod will serve as your handle as you build the cane. Heat it to molten and fuse it to the cane by pushing it onto the end of the cane while it's sitting in the kiln. Use preheated tweezers

> **NOTE**
>
> *Canes can be picked up with the end of a molten glass rod or tweezers. It's a good idea to work on this technique by practicing while the kiln and canes are cool.*

to help you manipulate the cane (photo 1). If you're using a smaller cane that's been warmed in the flame, push it into the molten end of the handle rod (photo 2).

As with the other cane masses, build this kind of cane from the inside out. To begin building, use a glancing flame to heat one side of your first cane element (the one with the handle) to a dull orange glow. Use tweezers to bring a second cane out of the kiln. Align the second cane along the glowing area and push the two together, beginning at the handle end of the first cane (photo 3). Use a graphite paddle to nudge the canes together so that they touch along their entire length (photo 4). (It's also possible to "float" canes in the background glass, leaving space around them. To do this, you'll surround or encase the cane with background glass before placing the second cane, and so on.)

Heat the background color rod until it is very molten. In a glancing flame, hold the rod at an angle (to avoid trapping air bubbles) and push the glass along the crevice between the two canes (photo 5). Be sure to use a glancing flame so that the rest of the cane stays firm.

Using this technique, you can add as many cane elements as your design calls for, filling in crevices as needed.

As you add canes, you can leave a trough between two canes and push the next cane snugly into this spot, adding it from the handle end to the tip of the cane so that you don't create air channels.

When you've added all the canes, encase the whole design. Add handles and pull the cane out as previously described. When pulling this cane down, don't pull it until it is so small that the images are

visually ineffective when sliced and added to a bead.

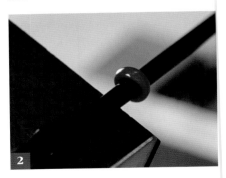

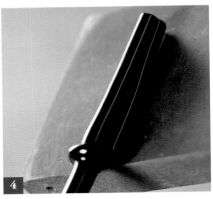

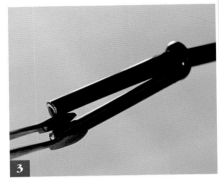

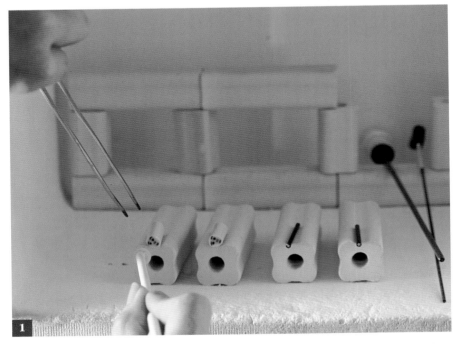

Color Mixing

Even though there are many colors of glass available in rod form, it's great to be able to combine various colors to create darker or lighter shades or add a tinge of a certain color to another one. These mixed colors are often used to create shaded areas in a face cane and other picture canes. You'll definitely need to experiment—and you won't always get the results that you expect! (For instance, since black is actually a very dark purple, mixing white with it will make it purple, not gray.)

Keep in mind that mixing glass is not like mixing paint. Some colors will end up looking like mud, so keep a log of what works and doesn't work together.

To mix glasses, begin by heating the ends of the two rods of different color at the torch simultaneously. Push them together in the flame, and then swirl and spin them (photo 1). Continue to mix them until the rope-like lines disappear from the glass. As you do this, don't push more glass into the molten area.

Bring the glass out of the flame and and pull it into a very thick stringer. Hold the stringer straight for a few seconds so that you'll have a fairly straight rod. Let it cool

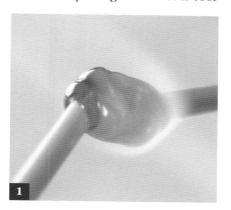

a bit and check the resulting color. It's possible to reheat the glass and add more of one of the initial colors if you weren't able to get the shade that you want. When you're done, place the stringer on the tabletop and cut away the mixing rods with nippers.

To create a group of shades ranging from light to dark (or vice versa), leave a small amount of the mixed color on the mixing rods after the first pull of new color. Mix that color again to create a lighter or darker version.

Creating a Portrait with Facial Elements

Canes representing facial elements can be combined to make intriguing portraits. Each facial element is built separately before it is drawn down to a smaller size. You can imagine the possibilities for this art—the faces that you can portray are virtually endless in terms of individual coloring, the shape of features, and even the expression.

This is a complicated technique, and it will take you a lot of time and practice to begin to master. However, it can be absolutely amazing when you pull your first successful portrait cane and see the results in sliced cameo form. These tiny portrait canes can then be applied to beads as delightful surface decoration.

Before you begin your portrait, you'll make a sketch and divide the face into its most basic elements of the eyes, nose, and mouth. Once these features are built and pulled out to about the same diameter (so that they relate proportionally), they're combined into a face cane.

Once this larger cane is pulled out, you can add details such as the eyebrows, hair, a neckline, or jewelry before you pull the final cane.

In the section that follows, we'll begin by describing how to make the separate features before we tell you how to combine them into a face. Anneal each element before going to the next stage of adding it to the larger cane.

MAKING AN EYE CANE: Study figure 1 below that shows how to build a basic eye cane with numbers indicating the order of assembly. Notice that the iris isn't perfectly round because the eyelid blocks the top portion of it, so you'll need to pay attention to this as you build it.

Begin with a dark rod to serve as the eye's pupil. Case the rod with a color representing the iris. Keep painting on glass, and take a look at the end of the rod to gauge what you're doing as you build the shape. Smooth and shape this portion of the cane on a marver as needed.

To create the whites of the eyes, use white glass to build triangular wedges on each side of the iris, creating an elliptical shape. The whites determine the overall shape of the eye. Skim on a very thin coating of dark brown around the entire ellipse to lend definition to it.

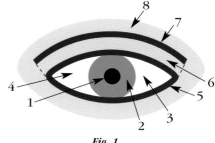

Fig. 1

151

Next, add skin color on top of the eye. Details at the top of the eye can be varied. (Eyelashes aren't impossible, but they can be difficult to see when the cane is drawn down, so you might find them a waste of time.) Add a skin crease above this area to give the eye more definition. You'll add eyebrows later when you assemble the portrait. Encase the cane with a final layer of skin color before adding handles and pulling it.

As you heat the cane mass, it naturally begins to round off and lose its elliptical shape. Therefore, add extra glass at the edges or corners of the eye when adding handles so that the glass supports this area when the cane is heated. Avoid shooting a lot of heat directly at the corners on either end of the eye, since these are thinner and more vulnerable to slumping out of shape as you're heating the cane. Instead, concentrate the flame in the mid-section of the cane mass. Retain the curves of the shape during heating by rocking the mass back and forth on your graphite paddle or torch-top marver, pushing the heat toward the center of the mass.

MAKING A NOSE CANE: Study figure 2 before you begin making the nose cane. From this basic idea, you can vary the shape of the nose to make it longer, straighter, wider, or even crooked.

To make the nose, surround a skin color rod with glass of the same color to form the bridge of the nose. Skim dark brown along one side of the oval bridge. Then add more skin color along both sides of the bottom to create rounded nostrils. Use a rounded-edge paddle to shape the nostrils at the bottom. After the shape is formed, you can skim-coat areas with dark brown glass or use a mixed color (see the section on color mixing on page 151) to add definition or shading. If you want to add a moustache, you can add it to the bottom of the nose now, or leave the skin layer thin on the bottom of the nose so that you can add it later.

Encase the cane in skin color so that it is rounded, before adding handles and pulling it out. Again, keep the diameter size in mind as you pull so that it's proportional to the eyes.

MAKING A MOUTH CANE: Study figure 3 that shows the parts of the mouth cane. From this starting point, you can vary the mouth as you wish to create different expressions or make the lips fuller or narrower.

Begin by forming the top lip, a long ellipse, around a central rod of the same color. Use a rounded graphite paddle to indent the top of it. Add a very thin line of black at the bottom of the top lip to divide it from the bottom lip or use white to represent teeth. Then add the rounded lip at the bottom. Shape and smooth the entire mouth carefully before encasing it in skin color.

Like the eye, this shape is elliptical, so keep that in mind when it comes time to pull it out. Build the handles with extra glass at the edges as you did on the eye cane, and avoid heating the thin edges, since they're vulnerable to distortion. Retain the curves of the shape during heating by rolling the mass on your graphite paddle or torch-top marver.

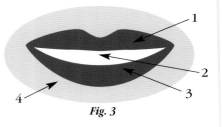

Fig. 3

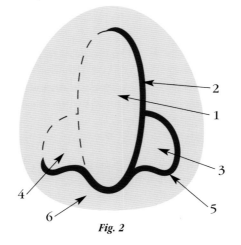

Fig. 2

Constructing the Face

You'll assemble the face in the same way that you did the complex cane described earlier. Nip the canes into equal lengths of about 1¼ (3.2 cm) inches each. Line up the canes in the kiln to preheat them, along with extra sections in case you need them. You'll be assembling the eyes, nose, and mouth, or the essential components of the face into one cane. When you reach the stage of completing the portrait (adding the hair and so forth), you have the option of adding more glass to make the face rounder, longer, or some other shape.

The nose will form the center of the cane. Attach a handle rod to the preheated nose cane and take it out of the kiln to warm it in the flame. Add skin color beneath the nose, forming in the upper lip. Next, add the mouth cane and add skin color around it and beneath it to fill out the lower portion of the face and part of the chin. Add the cheeks, defining them by using a lighter mixed color if you wish. Then add one eye cane, and fill in around it. Add the other eye cane, and fill in around it.

Add the eyebrows above the eyes, using a small line of color. Add a small amount of skin color above the brows, but keep the forehead narrow at this point so that you have the option of being creative with the shape of it at the final portrait stage.

Add handles to the cane mass, heat it to molten, and pull it out to a relatively large diameter (at least ½ inch [1.3 cm]) so that it's easier to see and work with as you complete the portrait cane. Anneal the cane.

Completing a Portrait Cane

Read through the following section to give you some basic steps for completing a portrait. When you come up with your own ideas, make sure to draw a sketch to follow as you work.

To begin completing the portrait, nip the annealed face cane into 1¼ inch (3.2 cm) lengths. Place them in the kiln to preheat. If you're working with a sketch of your own, choose your colors for each section and have plenty of rods of color on hand.

Pick up the preheated cane with tweezers and attach a molten rod to it to serve as the handle for the larger cane (photo 1). Place the cane in the flame to warm it.

If needed, use skin color to fill out the chin. You can add a medium brown line to define the bottom of the chin, or you can use a mixed color (photo 2). Fill in the neck area with the skin color or a lighter mixed color to get the shape you want (photo 3).

Add a thin layer of black to suggest a necklace (photo 4) and a star cane or other cane with a small design in it to form a pendant.

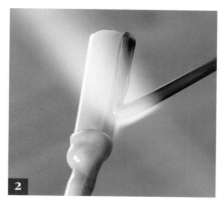
1

3

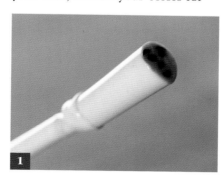
2

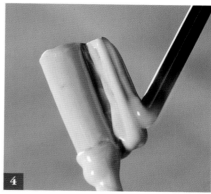
4

Then fill in with more skin color below it (photo 5). Add a circular-colored shape beneath this to emulate a garment and serve as the bottom of the image (photo 6).

Now you'll finish the top of the portrait. Shape the forehead with skin-colored glass, leaving the top so that it can accommodate the hair's shape. Add the hair to the top

NOTE

To avoid thermal shock, remember to occasionally bathe the entire cane mass with heat so that it stays warm throughout as you work on particular sections.

of the head. You can use a rounded graphite paddle to put ridges in the hair, suggesting curls or waves (photo 7). Fill in the background color around the hair to create a rounded cane (photo 8).

Because of the volume of glass in this cane, use soft glass cones and sturdier borosilicate handles to pull it. Nip the borosilicate handles away as soon as the glass rigidifies to remove the incompatible glass and the possibility of splitting the cane. Cut the cane into short sections before annealing it in the kiln.

Cutting Slices of Cane

Canes can be nipped into slices with tile nippers purchased from a hardware store. Hold the cane so that it is nipped as evenly as possible (photo 1). You can cut slices of any thickness, depending on your design and how you plan to use the cane. If your cane has an outer design on it, remember to nip it slightly longer since the design will close in a bit at the top when heated, spread out at the bottom, and show the design surrounding it.

Thicker cane is difficult to nip with tile nippers. You can use a wet tile saw with a fine, diamond-embedded blade to cut even slices. You will, however, lose some of the cane when you grind it with the blade.

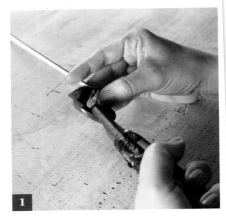

Making Floral Beads

DEANNA GRIFFIN DOVE

Around a quarter of a million species of flowers inhabit our world. Each possesses unique botanical characteristics. Many of these flowers have symbolic meanings or associations such as the coming of spring, the celebration of love, or the comfort of mourners. It is no wonder they inspire artists and craftspeople.

All flowers are rich in detail, texture, and form. Thus, it is challenging to reproduce them in glass—a viscous material that, once applied, is difficult to erase. In this section we'll cover various techniques, from the simplest to more complex. These techniques can be used to make petals and stems or combined to construct flowers. Even simple dot techniques can make lovely flowers. Raking techniques elongate dots into petals and leaves. In advanced techniques, you'll commingle glass canes that you've made to produce subtle hue shifts and delicate veins.

To make flowers you'll need a large variety of canes. Preparing each detail of a flower (centers, petals, and stems) with a unique cane will ensure beautiful results. The three beads that follow show different ways of applying and manipulating varied canes. As you advance in knowledge, you can use more complex canes while making your flowers more colorful and your beads more unique.

Pulling Floral Canes

Before you build floral canes, you must understand how to pull them down to a smaller diameter. (An average floral cane is about 1 mm.) After you've built the cane, add a rod to serve as a handle at the opposite end, leaving the rod you've been using attached. Heat up the cane mass and shape it by focusing heat at both ends, allowing each to smooth out and taper (photo 1). Continue to heat the entire mass (including the ends) until molten and the same temperature throughout—indicated by an even-colored orange glow with no hotspots or darker, cool spots.

When everything is evenly heated, take the cane mass out of the flame and pause a few seconds to allow the exterior to cool slightly. Begin pulling the cane very slowly. The tapered ends of the cane should pull out first, drawing increasingly more glass from the interior of the mass. These thinner end sections will cool and set up. (If you notice the center thinning and pulling out before the ends, this indicates an unevenly heated cane mass.)

1

Increase your rate of pull *only* when the thinnest part of the cane has started to set up and the cane is slightly thicker than desired. Hold the cane steady at the end of the pull. Although you can't continue pulling, the cane will still be bendable. Once it has stiffened, flame-cut or cut it with tile nippers into 10-inch (25.4 cm) lengths.

Making Floral Canes

The following section covers some cane variations that work well for floral decoration. Cased cane and striped, or ribbed, cane are your basic building blocks, along with stringers and twisted cane. Each of these types of cane can be used lengthwise to make linear forms. They can be pushed onto the bead to paint on petal forms, or their cross-section can be used to create flower centers.

Colorful examples of ribbed cane

Encased Cane

This kind of cane has many applications for floral beads because the transparent encasing protects the line created by the interior color. This means that you can place encased canes side-by-side or coil the cane to create multiple lines or patterns. (In contrast, if you tried this with a stringer, the glass would flow together, creating a solid color.)

The encasing also keeps the interior colors from spreading. You can also create lines of different thicknesses, depending on the ratio of the inside color to the outside color.

The following variations will add interest and distinction to your flowers. This list is meant only to jump-start your explorations. Look at real petals to inspire your color combinations. Use high contrast colors to make a statement about line or use related colors to create texture.

⚜ If you're encasing an opaque rod with transparent color, you can apply more than one color to create a variegated effect. Change color as you work your way around the rod. For example, try using three shades of transparent amethyst around a dark rose/pink core. This particular combination creates depth through an illusion of shadow.

⚜ Vary the thickness of the encasing color to fit the cane's purpose. To increase the thickness, simply add another layer on top of the first one. For example, to represent a flower's stamen, a thickly encased cane can be used to distinctly depict each filament. A stamen can be drawn on the bead separately, or a larger cane can be built from multiple cased canes and pulled out to create a more complex center. A very thin casing keeps stems separated from the background without intruding on the overall design. Also, it's easier to control the casing by striping it on at a sharp angle.

> **NOTE**
>
> *Flip back to chapter 3 (page 63) and reread the section on encasing stringers. The same encasing technique applies to floral canes.*

⚜ Encase the core completely with more than one color to mix new or different colors. For example, encase a white rod with transparent blue and then add a layer of transparent amethyst for a bluish purple color.

⚜ Encase a pastel or transparent core rod with another pastel or transparent color and use the resulting cross-section (sliced cane) as flower centers.

⚜ Using frit or enamel powders gives you more color possibilities for various flowers. Roll the core rod in a generous layer of either material. Heat the frit or powder to molten and roll it on a graphite paddle to smooth out the surface before encasing it in a transparent color.

Striped Floral Cane

In the following section we'll show you a couple of ways to make striped/ribbed canes, probably the most useful cane for flowers. (You can also make striped cane using an optic mold, as we described previously.

Stripes can be added to the outside of a core color, or the core can be indented with a knife-edged tool before pushing the stripes into valleys. The first technique is quicker and easier, but the second yields a crisper look because the stripes don't spread out on the surface of the cane when it's heated. Of course, the color combinations are endless, but the basic idea is to use an opaque interior or core color with contrasting stripes. While either opaque or transparent colors can be used for the stripes, transparent stripes will give a look of depth while opaque colors are more obvious and distinct. If you want to encase the stripes, you'll need a transparent or clear rod.

To use the first technique, heat the core rod to molten, forming a large ball at the end. Angle the rod upward so that the glass flows down onto the rigid part of the rod as it heats to molten. Shape the glass into a barrel shape by rolling it on a graphite paddle, creating a thick section on which to work. Or, encase the core rod in the same color, adding several layers until the section is approximately 1/2 inch (1.3 cm) in diameter before smoothing and rounding it with a graphite paddle.

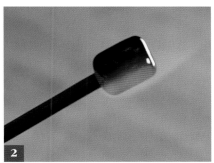

Use fat stringers to add stripes of color down the length of the thicker core section. Apply the stringers so that they connect with one another on the top end of the core, ensuring that the stripes pull out evenly. Add stripes around the core, being careful to keep them from touching (photo 1). Add a handle rod at the end of the cane and pull it out as previously described.

To use the second technique, create a thick core. With a glancing flame selectively heat one area of the core (photo 2). Take it out of the flame and push a knife-edged tool into the length of it, wiggling it back and forth a little to create a narrow valley (photo 3). Make indentations all the way around the core (photo 4). Push the contrasting stringers into and along the length of the valleys (photo 5). Again, the stringers should meet at the end of the cane. Add a handle, and evenly heat the cane mass, pulling it out as before.

There are many variations of striped cane and some are quite complex. This cane is invaluable for

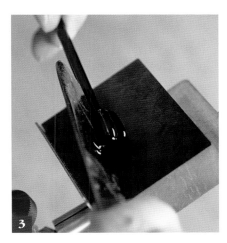

creating texture and detail. Striped cane is used mainly for depicting petals, but it's also useful for making leaves, stems, and seed balls.

Use strong hues for highly saturated color. Create veins with the visible stripes. Use transparent stripes for delicate textural effects. If you create a group of these striped canes, following the suggestions below, you'll have a good stock of canes to use for many purposes.

❧ Alternate stripes of various colors.

❧ Add another transparent color on top of each stripe to create another color.

❧ Add another pastel color to create stripes within stripes.

❧ Use a smooth pastel-colored barrel shape as your core. Add pastel stripes to it. Smooth the first layer of stripes with a graphite paddle and add another of transparent so that it overlaps partially on the pastel stripe and partially on the core color. This will create a gradation between stripe and core.

❧ Use cased cane or filigrana stringers for your stripes. A filigrana core with more filigrana stripes is excellent to use as stamen cane.

❧ Use aventurine for the stripes to create a delicate glitter in the resulting cane.

❧ Encase the entire mass in a transparent color prior to pulling it out.

❧ Begin with a core of bullseye cane or a millefiori cane and add stripes to it to make wonderful flower centers.

Flat Cane

Flat cane can be a bit tricky to keep in shape as it's pulled, but it's ideal to use for leaves and long petals. When applied to a bead, it can be folded over as it's laid down to produce some very natural looking effects.

To make a flat cane, heat a rod of opaque glass (usually green for leaves) to molten and form a large ball of molten glass. Use a parallel press to flatten the gather into a rectangular shape, working back and forth (top to side) to disperse the glass (photo 1). Flatten it as much as possible (less than $^1/_8$ inch [3 mm]). This is difficult to do because the tool cools the glass as soon as it touches the surface of it. You'll need to reheat the paddle and press it again to make it thinner.

Choose a second color in stringer form that is slightly lighter or darker than the paddle to use as a stripe down the center, suggesting a stem (photo 2). Hold the rectangular paddle parallel and to the side of the flame with the stringer slightly above it so that it softens up. Paint it down the middle, and heat it so that it's fused well but left as a ridge.

Add a handle rod to the end of the cane. Hold the flat side of the rectangle to the flame and heat it carefully until it's molten. Flip the cane, but don't rotate it (photo 3). (Rotating the cane will make it round out.) Once the mass is thoroughly heated to a dull orange glow, pull as you would any other cane (photo 4).

There are several variations possible with flat cane, including the following:

❧ Apply thin stripes of a similar or contrasting color on one side of the rectangle, covering it completely. Use a parallel press to mash the glass again. Add a center stripe to this side. When it's made into a finished cane, each side will be a different color. This cane works wonderfully to create realistic shading, such as the darker sides of leaves.

❧ Contrasting stripes of color can be added to the edges of the rectangle to create a leaf with more variation.

❧ To create an illusion of depth in the resulting cane, add two transparent stripes to each side of the center stripe. Melt the stripes in and flatten them again with the parallel press before pulling the cane out.

❧ Make a cased or striped cane and flatten it into a rectangle before pulling it.

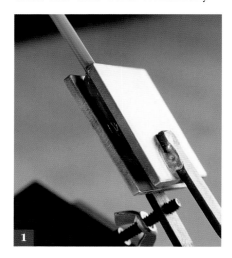

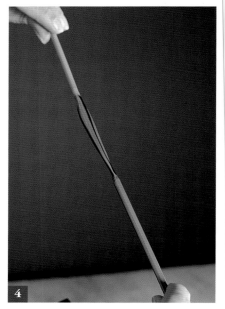

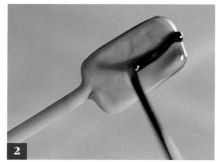

Creating the Flowers

This section will introduce you to the art of combining various techniques to make beautiful flowers. Keep in mind that we're only scratching the surface of what's possible! We'll cover the basic techniques of using dots and dot patterns and altering the dots with a rake. Then, we'll give you a close look at how to create flower petals, leaves, and other details with special strokes.

Take time to think through the design of your bead to determine the order of added details. If you place larger objects first, it makes it easier to figure out the spacing for smaller elements. For instance, sometimes the flower will be the largest part of your design, so you have to gauge how much space is left for the placement of leaves and vines. Usually, you'll place leaves last, but not always. Sometimes stems are placed before flowers because it's easier to overlap the edge of the stem with a petal than try to push the stem underneath it.

> ## NOTE
> *You'll notice an extra bead near the tip of the mandrel in the photos beginning on page 160. Make this "junk" bead immediately after making the base bead by using a little bit of your base bead color to wrap a tiny bead. Don't worry about the shape of it. This bead can serve as a repository for excess glass, or as glass from which to pull the end of a cane or stringer into a sharp tip.*

Using Dots to Create Wisteria and Dogwood

In some parts of the country, wisteria vines engulf dogwood trees and bloom at the same time. Both of these floral forms can be depicted with simple dot techniques.

Use an off-centered bicone as your base bead, since the form mirrors the triangular tendrils of wisteria blossoms. Wrap a long slender bead and shape it carefully with a graphite paddle. (The bead pictured is made of transparent medium blue with the addition of transparent medium amethyst and transparent cobalt.) Shape and center the bead (photo 1).

Use a twisted cane made of two shades of light brown to add the wisteria vines to the bead. Hold the bead slightly below the flame with the twist to the side of it, allowing it to soften as you draw with it on the bead. Apply the vines in an upside-down L-shape (photo 2) around the bead (three were added to this bead). Gently heat and fuse the vines to the base bead without melting them in flush.

To create dogwood blossoms, use a fat stringer of a pale pink opaque glass. At the four points of a square, place four dots close together without touching. Place several groups of dots around the bead. While they're hot, press each group of dots with a marver to flatten them (photo 3). To alter the shape of each dot, heat it with a pinpoint flame, and place the point of a rake at the outside edge (not directly on the dot). Push towards

the center of the grouping (photo 4). The group of dots will begin to look like a dogwood flower. Use a cased cane (light yellow over transparent green) to add three to five very small dots in the center of each flower (photos 5 and 6).

Next you'll represent wisteria blossoms made up of tiny flowers hanging in bunches from the vines. To represent these cascading blossoms, use striped cane made of light sky-blue stripes over dark blue (photo 7). Add dots on top of dots, creating depth and dimension as you work your way up the bead, crossing over the vines (photo 8). After you're done, fuse them to the base bead by heating them gently in the flame, leaving some of the dimensional detail.

To add leaves, as shown in the finished bead, use a green stringer to place dots around the bead. Reheat each dot and push a knife-edged tool across it to indent each leaf, depicting the center vein.

Using Dots to Create Daffodils and Wildflowers

You can use a small-tipped stringer as a raking tool to create very elegant, detailed shapes. To create a sharp point on a larger stringer strong enough to do the raking without breaking off on the bead, place the molten stringer on your "junk" bead and pull it away (photo 1), leaving a hair-like extension of glass at the end of the stringer. After making the extension, push it straight down on your work surface, breaking off any glass that is too thin to do the raking (photo 2).

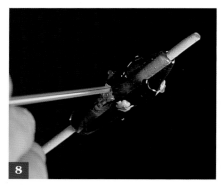

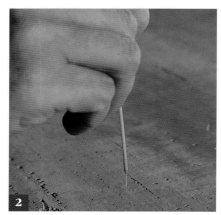

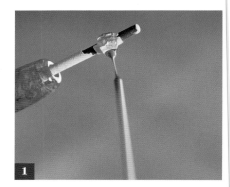

160

The base bead used for this group of flowers is a long tube-shaped bead of pale aqua glass, trailed with threads of cased cane made of pastel green. The bead is cased with clear glass and pulled out very thin. Trail the canes across the bead diagonally.

You can suggest wildflowers by laying down five dots in a circle with a coral or other light-colored stringer. To evenly place the five dots, place three dots at the points of an imaginary isosceles triangle before bisecting the long sides of the triangle with the final two dots (photo 3). Create more flowers around the bead. Point a pinpoint flame at the center of each circle of dots and melt them in all the way (photo 4). As the glass becomes molten, surface tension will draw the inner edges of the dots toward the middle to make triangular-shaped petals. Plunge a cased cane (yellow cased with dark red) into the center of these petals (photo 5). Snap the cane away after it cools a bit. It should break just below the surface of the bead. Concentrate the flame on the flower until the surface is flush.

To make daffodils, use a stringer to place six yellow dots in a circle. To place them evenly, form an equilateral triangle with three dots and bisect each side with the remaining three dots. Make a sharp point on your yellow stringer as previously described, using your "junk" glass at the end of the mandrel. Heat a dot with a pinpoint flame and place your raker/stringer at the inside edge of each dot and pull towards the center of the group (photo 6). Your stringer will probably stick to the bead. When it does, break it loose from each dot, blow a quick puff of air where the tip is attached to cool it down, and then snap it loose. After pulling each dot to the center, gently heat each one again and pull outward from the outer edge to form a petal (photo 7). Repeat this process on the other flowers.

Use a light yellow stringer to place a dot in the center of each group of six petals, filling the flower's center. While the dot is hot, plunge a rake into the center of it to form the daffodil cup (photo 8).

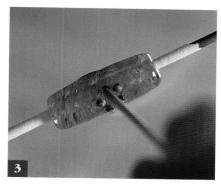

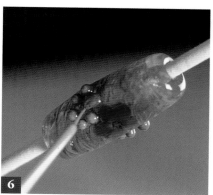

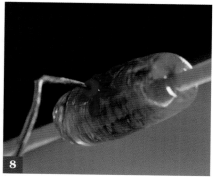

To make smaller flowers, heat the tip of a striped cane (stripes of white on an orange base). Attach it to the "junk" glass bead, pull away slightly (photo 9), and flame-cut it to create a point on the end, bringing all of the stripes on the cane together. Now heat a small ball of glass to molten at the end of this cane, keeping the ball centered. Press the ball straight onto the bead so that the stripes spread out (photo 10). Flame-cut the

striped cane 1/4 inch (6 mm) away from the bead, leaving a tail of glass behind (photo 11).

Hold the bead so that the tail is pointed down. Heat only the tail. Carefully remove it by pulling it with a tweezers so that all the cane stripes are drawn together (photo 12). Flame-cut the tiny bit of remaining glass. Press the dot flat so that it spreads out slightly (photo 13). Repeat this step to make more small flowers.

Using Strokes to Create Irises, Peonies, and Roses

Strokes with glass are similar to painting. However, you're using an entirely different medium. To capture the fluidity of the iris petal, for instance, your glass must be molten or fluid.

The shape of a petal or leaf can be manipulated even after it's laid down. You can use a stringer to pull molten glass from the edge or use a knife-edged tool to push glass from under the edge of a petal or leaf to adjust its shape.

Before you begin painting details on beads with stringers and canes, create a point at the end of the stringer or cane by touching the molten tip to your "junk" bead at the end of the mandrel. Pull it away and flame-cut the point. Immediately touch this point down on the bead without going back into the flame since the point still carries enough heat to stick to the

9

10

11

12

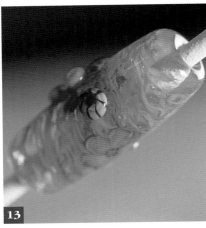

13

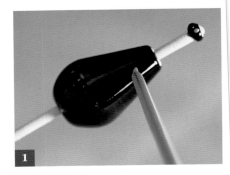

1

NOTE

Keep in mind that stringers and canes will gather into a ball as soon as they're introduced into the flame, making it a challenge to lay down a pointed cane to add flower details.

bead (photo 1). Then continue with the stroke.

Begin with a teardrop-shape base bead in dark brown to contrast with lightly colored irises, peonies, and roses. Make sure that the base bead is shaped exactly as desired before beginning the floral decorations.

IRIS: To make the long fluid leaves of an iris, you can use a striped flat green cane laid down in long strokes that begin at the top of the leaf and flow to the bead's base. Soften the cane in the top of the flame with the bead at the side of the flame. Pull the cane away as you flame-cut it, tapering the end for the next stroke.

Begin the stroke again, but about halfway down the stem, flip the cane over as it's being laid down to simulate a folded leaf (photo 2). Continue to the base of the bead and flame-cut the cane. Roll a round graphite rod over the leaf to flatten it and make sure that the tip of the leaf is well connected to the base bead and retains its shape (photo 3).

For a different style of background leaves, use a green stringer to make a grouping of five dots in the shape of a leaf (place four dots to form a square and then add a dot at the top). Heat the dots until they're almost flush with the bead (photo 4). Rake through the grouping with a green stringer, beginning at the top dot and continuing between the other dots to the base of the leaf (photo 5). This action will pull all the dots together, suggesting a leaf with lobes.

To form the stem, pull a point on a green stringer and draw a long line, beginning where you anticipate adding an iris blossom and continuing to the base of the leaves. Curve it slightly to indicate motion.

The iris blossom has several parts, including the upright *standards* and the lower *falls*. To form the petals, begin by heating the end of your striped cane and gently pulling all the stripes to a point from the "junk" glass bead. This will ensure that the stripes are laid out evenly on the bead.

You'll be adding three standard petals: two next to one another and a third on top that partially covers them. To form the two back standards, heat a small ball to molten before pressing the gather onto the bead with a C-shaped stroke (photo 6). Pull it away from the bead and flame-cut the cane. Repeat this stroke for the other standard with a reversed C-shape, overlapping a bit of the first standard (photo 7).

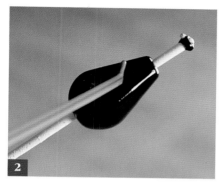

2

3

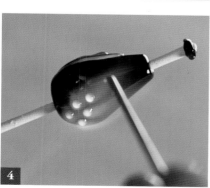

4

5

6

7

Next make a scalloped stroke by pressing the molten ball into the standards, pushing up (away from the base or center of the flower) to the top of the petal before pulling back past the middle. This motion will cause the stripes to fan out at the top of the stroke (photo 8).

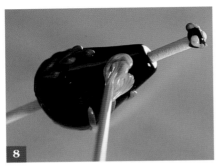

Flame-cut the cane at the center of flower (at the meeting point of the two back standards). If the bottom of the standard is bulky, spot-heat this section and pick off the extra glass with tweezers (photo 9).

To create the falls, pull molten glass once again from the tip of your cane to pull all the stripes to the end. Form a small ball of molten glass at the end of the cane. Attach the ball below and to the left of the flower center, and pull towards the center (photo 10). Repeat this stroke for the other fall.

There will be a larger mass of glass where the petals were flame-cut at the center, so spot-heat this mass with a pinpoint flame, keeping the tips of the petals stiff. Take the bead out of the flame and use tweezers to pull off the mass (photo 11). Flame-cut the mass afterwards. This action will pull the petals into a small graceful point at

the flower's center. Use a pick to push in the center of the flower (photo 12).

PEONIES: To make peonies with multiple overlapping petals, use a cased cane (dark blue over light pink). With a small ball of molten glass, make a short stroke that begins at the outer tip of one of the petals, drawing it in to the center of the flower. Flame-cut the cane. Add three more petals, creating a fan shape (photo 13). Add two shorter strokes on top of these strokes

(photo 14, previous page). Flame-cut the end of each stroke.

As on the previous flower, repeated flame-cutting at the same spot leaves a bulk of glass at the end point. Focus a pinpoint flame at this spot and pull this glass away with tweezers before flame-cutting it. Heat a small ball of green stringer and place it over the elongated point. Continue drawing with the stringer straight down to the bottom of the bead to create the stem (photo 15, previous page).

ROSES: You can make lovely roses using a cased cane (such as dark rose cased with gold-pink) to draw a concentric coil around the point where you first touch down the cane. The tighter you make this coil, the more realistic the flower looks (photo 16). Use a rake and push the coils in toward the center at various points to create the illusion of individual petals (photo 17).

16

17

Top: Becky Schupbach
Leaf Necklace, 2003
2.5 x 1.6 cm (leaves)
Lampworked; soda-lime glass
Photo by Geoffrey Carr

Center left: Sylvus Tarn
Triple Hollow Beads, 2003
2.5 x 3.2 x 3.2 cm
Lampworked; soda-lime glass;
surface trailing
Photo by artist

Center right: Kimberly Jo Affleck
Baroque Cascade Opal, 2003
9.52 x 1.27 x 1.27 cm
Soft glass; silver fume
Photo by Roger Schreiber

Bottom: Ann Davis, *Pele's Tears*, 2004
2.5 cm diameter
Lampworked with electroformed center;
soda-lime glass; dicro stringer and patina
Photo by Jeff O'Dell

165

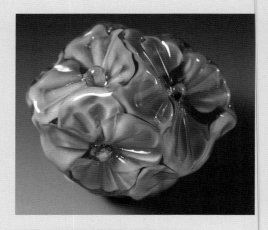

Top left: Karen Moyer, *Pamlynn,* 2002
5 x 3.5 x 4 cm
Lampworked in oxygen/propane torch and
shaped with dental and manicurist tools;
soda-lime glass
Photo by Brian McLernon

Top center: Patsy Evins
Floral Garden, 2004
4.3 x 2.1 x 2 cm
Lampworked; soda-lime glass; encased;
striped stringer
Photo by Dennis Evins

Top right: Lea Zinke, *Hydrangea Bead,* 2003
2.5 cm diameter
Lampworked; soda-lime glass; surface embellishment
Photo by Jerry Mesmer

Bottom left: Kristen Frantzen Orr, *Nouveau Again,* 2003
5.4 x 1.27 x 1.27 cm
Lampworked; soft glass; goldstone inclusions, partially
etched, and surface florals created with multi-layered,
striped cane
Photo by David Orr

Bottom center: Deanna Griffin Dove
Golden Haze from the Requiem Series, 2003
3.8 x 1.9 cm
Lampworked; gold reduction frit; pick techniques
to elongate petal shapes
Photo by artist

Bottom right: Patsy Evins, *Tropic Flip Flop,* 2004
3.4 x 1.6 x 1.5 cm
Lampworked; soda-lime glass; twistie stringer, stacked dots,
and etched
Photo by Dennis Evins

Top left: Kate Fowle Meleney
Green Hydra, 2004
7.5 x 2 cm
Lampworked; soda-lime glass; silver
and copper leaf, electroformed copper,
liver of sulfur patina
Photo by Jerry Anthony

Top right: Debby Yabczanka
Emerald Isle, 2003
2 x 1.5 x 2 cm (largest)
Lampworked; soda-lime glass; stringer,
reduction frit, and sterling silver accents
Photo by Jim Swallow

Center left: Fujie Kawata
Rose, 2003
2.3 x 2.7 x 2.7 cm
Lampworked; lead and soda-lime glass;
24-karat gold foil
Photo by artist

Center right: Marjorie Burr
Relics, 2003
2.7 x 1.1 x 2.7 cm (right);
3.3 x 1.8 x 1.3 cm (left)
Lampworked; electroformed copper
Photo by Roger Schreiber

Bottom left: Sara Hoyt, *Sumi-e,* 2004
1.8 x 1.8 x 1 cm
Lampworked; soda-lime glass; layered
dots, patterned cane, hand-built murrini,
and etched
Photo by artist

Bottom right: Marybeth Piccirelli
Sunrise & Sunset Butterflies, 2004
3.7 x 2.6 x 0.8 cm each
Lampworked; soda-lime glass; silverleaf
Photo by Tim Thayer

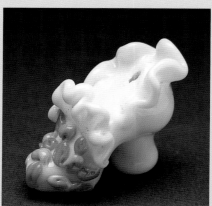

Top left: Lea Zinke
Garden Mini Beads, 2002
1.3 cm diameter
Lampworked; soda-lime glass; surface embellishment
Photo by Nancy Wieland

Top center: Mavis Smith, *Fairy Queen,* 2003
2.5 x 1.9 x 1.3 cm
Lampworked; soda-lime glass; twisted stringer, hand-made, encased murrine, sterling silver wire, and crystal accents
Photo by artist

Top right: Patricia Hoyt, *Lavender Angel,* 2000
3.3 x 7 x 1.9 cm
Lampworked; soda-lime and dichroic glass; enamel powders, stripe, and ribbon canes
Photo by Rich Images

Center left: Carolyn Noga
Fruit Lady, 2003
2.5 cm tall
Lampworked; soda-lime glass
Photo by Painter Photography

Center right: Karen Moyer, *Floral Vintage Shoe,* 2002
2.5 x 3 x 2 cm
Lampworked in oxygen/propane torch and shaped with paddle tweezers; soda-lime glass
Photo by Brian McLernon

Bottom: Lisa Kan
Le Fiore Vive Series, 2003
3.2 x 1.1 cm; 3.5 x 1.2 cm; 3.4 x 1.2 cm (left to right)
Lampworked; soda-lime glass; ribbon-striped cane and enamels
Photo by Azad

Top left: Brad Pearson, *Assorted Vessels,* 2003
Approximately 5 to 7.6 cm tall
Lampworked, hollow bead techniques; soda-lime glass
Photo by Taylor Dabney

Top right: Nancy Smith, Untitled, 2003
4.2 x 2.5 x 2 cm
Lampworked; soda-lime glass; hand-pulled stringer
Photo by Steve Gyurina

Center left: Patsy Evins, Untitled, 2004
Various dimensions
Lampworked; soda-lime glass; sculpted, encased, dots,
raked, stringer, and striped stringer
Photo by Dennis Evins

Center middle: Serena J.A. Smith, *Acrobat Bead,* 2002
7.6 x 3.8 x 2.5 cm
Lampworked; soft glass; sculpted with tweezers
Photo by artist

Center right: Pam Dugger, *Panther Grouper,* 2003
7.6 x 3.8 x 10.2 cm
Lampworked; soda-lime glass with borosilicate glass stand; sculpted, encased, and dots
Photo by Jeffrey O'Dell

Bottom left: Wendy Tobler, *U-Bead Bald Eagle with V-Bead American Flag,* 2003
5 x 8 x 2.2 cm
Freehand lampwork on triangle tool designed by artist; mandrel channels;
soda-lime glass
Photo by artist

Bottom right: Gladys J. Baez-Dickreiter, *Face Cane Cabochons,* 2002–2003
2.5 x 2.25 x 1 cm (gaspeite princess); 5 x 3.5 x 1 cm (rose queen);
2.5 x 2.5 x .75 cm (santa)
Lampworked; soda-lime glass; stringers, dots, ribbon colors, and sterling silver
bezel setting
Photo by artist

Troubleshooting Tips

PREVENTING THERMAL SHOCK
• If bits of glass pop off the end of the rod while you're heating it for the first time, heat the rod more slowly in the beginning and move the rod out to the cooler portion of the flame. • Some colors tend to shock more than others, including ones in the yellow/red/orange range as well as some yellowish greens. • Be sure to always put a hot rod down on a rod rest with the hot end suspended so that it has no contact with cooler rods and can cool evenly. • If a rod is put down directly on the tabletop or a marver, it will chill unevenly, resulting in stress that may cause thermal shock when it's reheated. • If a previously heated rod is cracked, the area will be prone to breaking when the rod is heated again, so heat it slowly and carefully. You can also break the cracked section off into your waste-glass container. The clean end might still contain stress and pop when heated, so heat it slowly. • When a short section of rod has been fused into a longer one, the fused area will probably contain stress. As you're using up the glass and approaching the fused area, move further out in the flame and heat it more gently to prevent thermal shock.

GLASS DOESN'T STICK TO MANDREL
• Make sure the mandrel is hot enough for the glass to stick. The glass, in turn, should be glowing orange and very molten. • The coated release must be completely dry. Rotate the mandrel in the flame to dry it out. After you dry out the release, make sure it's still intact, and then heat and begin again.

BEAD RELEASE BREAKS LOOSE FROM MANDREL
• If the release breaks loose as soon as the molten glass touches it, either the glass or mandrel aren't hot enough. Pull excess release off the rod with tweezers so that it's not mixed into your bead, and move to an area with intact release before preheating it and starting over. • If the release breaks while making a bead, the glass may have been too cool while being shaped. If the release repeatedly breaks loose, try to find a release brand with more tooth. • When using a graphite paddle to even up and shape a bead, do it carefully and gradually so that you don't break the release. • If there's release in the hot glass, it's possible to pluck it off the bead by heating the area and pulling it away with pointed tweezers. If the release is at the end of the bead around the mandrel, wait for the bead to cool, and try to file it off. If you plan to etch the bead, this will remove some of the release.

GLASS BECOMES GRAY, STREAKY, AND CLOUDY
• This means that the glass is burned, indicating that you're working too close to the cones or don't have the right mix of oxygen and propane. If working on a single-fuel torch, work further away from the blue cones and/or turn the flame down a bit. On a dual-fuel torch, make sure the cones are well defined. • Make sure the glass rod you use is clean and has no residue on it.

BUBBLES IN GLASS OR BEADS
• Since glass rod can boil when it is in the heat of the flame, bubbles can show up on the tip or surface of the rod. This is more prone to happen when the rod's end has been nipped, squared off, or pulled to a point, making the glass in this area very vulnerable. Use tweezers to pull off the bubbly glass before continuing to heat a bubble-free segment and wind the bead. • As you continue to heat glass and wind a bead, the glass may boil and bubble if held still and too close to the flame. Some colors, such as green, are more prone to this. • As always, make sure the glass is very clean.

BEADS HAVE UNWANTED TEXTURE
• If your beads are not smooth, they might have been too hot when you put them away to cool in the cooling blanket or vermiculite, leaving an impression behind.

BEAD BREAKS OR CRACKS AFTER COOLED TO ROOM TEMPERATURE
• When you flame-anneal the bead, wait for the glow to go away before placing it in a thermal blanket, vermiculite, or kiln. Don't let it get too cold. The glow is easier to judge in transparent glass than opaque glass. Hold the opaque bead under your tabletop, away from direct light, to check for an otherwise undetectable glow before putting it away. • Enamel powders have a lower melting temperature that soft glass. Give an enameled bead a few extra seconds to cool before putting it away.
• Evenly heat your bead before flame-annealing it. A hot spot on it will cause undue stress as the bead continues to cool, particularly when you cool the bead in a blanket or vermiculite. Placing the beads into a preheated annealing kiln alleviates this problem, since the bead soaks at a set temperature, allowing the temperature to even out throughout them before they cool. • If the bead contacts another hotter bead, it will create stress in the glass. Watch out when you put freshly flame-annealed beads in with others that have already begun to cool off in a blanket or vermiculite. In a preheated kiln this is less of a problem. • Check the shape of the bead to be sure that there's no portion of the glass thinner than the mandrel, since this area will cool a lot quicker than the rest of the bead, creating a stress point. This is less likely to happen if you're using a preheated kiln. • Beads that are larger than $1/2$ inch (1.3 cm) in diameter on some point along the mandrel, or beads that have extended parts (such

as wings, arms/legs, or handles), will naturally have thinner areas that cool more quickly than the thicker ones, creating stress in the glass. Place these beads, on their mandrels, in a preheated annealing kiln. •Make sure you haven't used incompatible glasses together in the same bead.

BEADS ARE DIFFICULT TO REMOVE OR WON'T COME OFF THE MANDRELS

•Be sure that the release is not too thick or thin and is evenly coated on the mandrel. Glass should never come in contact with the metal mandrel since it is too difficult to break loose. •When you're first learning to wrap a bead, it's possible to loosen the release if you push the firm part of the glass onto the mandrel or pull the bead a lot with the rod. Manipulating the bead too heavily with the marver can also loosen the release. If the glass is transparent, you'll be able to see if the release has broken loose. With opaque glass, you may not realize the problem until trying to remove the bead from the mandrel. •Don't overheat the release or it can deteriorate and get brittle, causing it to break loose while the bead is being shaped.

THE GLASS ROD BECOMES TOO SHORT TO HOLD AT THE TORCH

•As you're making beads and using up a glass rod, it will grow too short to hold at the torch comfortably. You can fuse shorter pieces to a longer rod. To do this, heat one end of each rod so that a small area is molten and push the molten ends together while out of the flame. Return this area to the flame and heat it until it is a smooth ball (photo 1). Bring it out of the flame and pull the rods apart so that the thickness is the same along the heated area (photo 2). Hold the fused rod steady and rotate it slightly to determine if it's straight. Straighten it if needed. Wait for the new rod to rigidify before placing it on a rod rest. Don't allow the hot area to touch the rest.

GLASS COLOR AND VARIOUS RESPONSES IN THE FLAME

A few soft glasses (with a COE of 104) have some special qualities that are explained below:

•Striking colors are colors in reds, yellows, oranges, and gold ruby (under various names) that are transparent when purchased and that strike or change to the color when the glass is cooled to annealing temperature and then reheated. You might see a bit more color change when the beads are annealed in a kiln. The colors can vary from batch to batch, and it can be hard to tell the colors that have not yet been struck apart. Therefore, heat the end of each rod to molten to identify the color (photo 3). Work the striking colors carefully in the flame, since they burn easily. If you overheat them, the color will darken or get cloudy. Gold ruby is particularly susceptible to burning, so use a light hand with it.

•Blues and greens are made with copper oxide as at least one of the colorants. Exposing the opaque colors to a reduction flame will bring the copper to the surface. Silver will show up on turquoise. In the opaque versions of several greens and turquoise, the copper oxide can be coaxed at the molten stage to respond in various ways to certain other colors. The most common reaction is a dark line at the seam. This reaction tends to happen when the colors have been exposed to an extended period of heating. The reaction can be avoided by using gentle heating and as little time in the flame as possible.

•In general, light opaque colors tend to spread out when applied to a bead. The edges of the opaque color will also bleed into other colors, leaving a soft line between them if a lot of heated is used on the bead. If you're using a stringer in one of these colors, you can avoid this by making an encased stringer. Anice white actually intensifies bleeding to neighboring colors when the bead is overheated. Experimenting with the colors over time will teach you what to expect from each one.

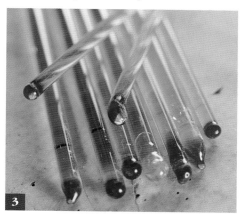

171

Ventilation Hood

Materials

2 sheets of 4 x 8-inch (10.2 x 20.3 cm) polyisocyanurate insulation board

4-inch (10.2 cm) wide aluminum tape

2 lengths of 1 x 3-inch (2.5 x 7.6 cm) wood board, each 4 feet (10.2 cm) long

Flexible insulated ducting, 6-inches (15.2 cm) in diameter (length needed depends on distance from hood to exhaust fan)

Straight register boot, with a 10 x 4-inch (25.4 x 10.2 cm) rectangular opening and 6-inch (15.2 cm) diameter opening for ducting attachment

4 bolts and nuts, each 3 inches (7.6 cm) long

4 fender washers, at least 1 inch (2.5 cm) in diameter

8 screw hooks, 2 inches (5 cm)

Chain for hanging hood from ceiling

Tools

Work gloves

Utility knife

Heavy-duty scissors

Drill with 3-inch (7.6 cm) bit

Screwdriver

Adjustable wrench or pliers

Instructions

Mark the full sheets of insulation board with measurements as shown in the diagram. Use a utility knife to score or slice the sections, two end pieces (A), two vertical sides (B), two angled sides (C), and one top section (D).

Cut a 10 x 4-inch (25.4 x 10.2 cm) centered hole in the top section (D), as shown in diagram 2. Use aluminum tape to secure the rectangular end of the straight register boot into the inside of this opening.

Align the two pieces of 1 x 3-inch (2.5 x 7.6 cm) wood board along each long edge of the top section (D) and tape them into place temporarily. Drill a total of four holes, approximately 2 inches (5 cm) in from the ends through both the wood and insulation. The holes should be the same diameter as the bolts.

Remove the wood boards from the top section (D) and set them aside. Screw in four screw hooks near the end of each board, being careful not to screw completely through. Set them aside.

Make a square, using the end sections (A) and the vertical sections (B) as shown in diagram 1. Note the placement of the vertical section in respect to the end section. The thickness of the vertical section should be visible at this joining. Tape all four corners on the inside and outside of the square.

Position both angled sections (C) on the vertical sections (B) and on the top edges of the end sections (A), as shown in diagram 1. The thickness of the angled sections (C) should be visible at the end. Tape along this area on the outside and inside of the hood.

Tape the top section (D) to the opening on the top of the hood (with the register boot already in place) along all four edges and on both inside and outside.

Place the wood boards on the top section (D), with the previously drilled holes aligned. Push the bolts through the holes from the top as shown in diagram 2. Turn the hood on its side to reach the interior. On the inside of the hood, slip a fender

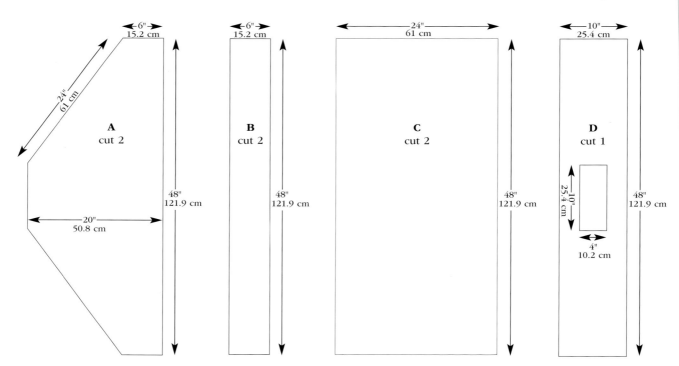

washer onto each bolt before adding the nut and tightening it using a screwdriver and adjustable wrench or pliers. Do not over tighten and crush the insulation board in any way.

While the hood is on its side, tape around all the bottom edges to cover any exposed insulation.

Set the hood upright again and slide one end of the 6-inch (15.2 cm) insulated ducting over the round end of the straight register boot and tape it in place.

Screw four screw hooks into the ceiling and support beams above your worktable. Place the hooks in a 4 x 4-foot (1.2 x 1.2 m) square so that the hood will hang centered over and slightly forward of the torch. Use sections of chain to hang the hood,

leaving only enough room to provide head clearance.

The other end of the insulated ducting is attached to the exhaust fan. The length of ducting needed will depend on the location of the hood in respect to the fan, which should be located at an exterior wall. See the diagram for a suggested set up (see page 28). If it is not possible to put the ducting through the ceiling, it will need to be supported by screwing it into the ceiling using sections of chain and screw hooks.

After the ducting is in place, check that the hood hangs horizontally. Make adjustments to the chains as needed.

The manner in which the ducting is attached to the exhaust fan will depend on the size of the fan and its intake opening. Another register boot may work, so ask for assistance at a home improvement store for the correct transition piece. Have an electrician wire the exhaust fan and power switch.

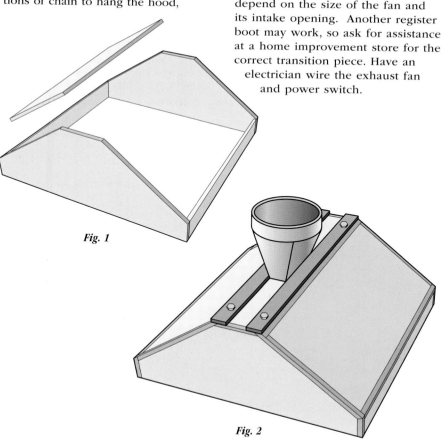

Fig. 1

Fig. 2

Acknowledgments

Many thanks to the following people:

To **Kathy** and **Jerry Catania** for starting me down this unexpected path

To **Cindy Jenkins** for being my first teacher and sharing information that contributed to the letter and number illustration on page 147

To my husband **Paul**, for allowing me to go down the path of my choice with lots of help and encouragement when I needed it, giving me room to do my own thing when the time came

To **Kate Fowle Meleney**—a great teacher and generous person—for her help and inspiration during the course of writing this book as well as the contribution of the book's sculptural section

To **Deanna Griffin-Dove** who encouraged and supported me during the writing of this book and whose expertise on florals took this book to a higher level

To **Jim Smirnich** for sharing the design of the arm rests shown on page 29

To **John Steinert** for contributing the optic molds pictured in the book

To all of my amazing teachers for being so open and generous with their time

To all of my students—from beginners at Camp Greystone to advanced artists at John C. Campbell Folk School—who keep me excited and motivated about sharing this amazing art form

To **Deborah Morgenthal** and **Carol Taylor** at Lark Books for giving me this opportunity to write this book

To art director **Kathy Holmes** whose eye and attention to detail made the book not only gorgeous but a pleasure to read and study

To **Keith Wright**, photographer, for fantastic photos that show the beauty and detail of working with the flame and molten glass

To **Katherine Aimone**, my editor, who has the patience of Job! Your support was unrelenting. Thank you for putting things in order and making the book read more clearly.

Glossary

Anice white glass: a white, soft glass that changes when exposed to a reduction flame

Annealing: slowly cooling glass through a certain temperature range in the kiln to relieve internal stress

Annealing kiln: an insulated kiln that allows you to control the temperature inside from room temperature to over 2000°F (1093°C)

Annealing temperature: the temperature at which the molecules vibrate enough to relieve stress in the glass over a period of time without being too hot to flow

Aventurine: glass in which metallic particles are suspended, simulating the gemstone, aventurine quartz

Bead release: a mixture of alumina and high-fire clay used to coat the mandrel so the bead can be removed after it cools

Black web or lace: surface decoration achieved through the use of intense black glass

Borosilicate (hard) glass: glass with a low coefficient of expansion, containing borax as flux that was originally formulated for making scientific equipment

Cane mass: volume of glass that contains the design of cane prior to being pulled down to a smaller diameter

Canes: thin rod, or groups of rods, which are combined at the torch in the molten state to create a design that is visible when seen in cross section or along its length

Check valve or flashback arrestor: a safety component that keeps the gas flowing away from the tank

Coefficient of expansion (COE): the degree to which a material expands and contracts at a fixed range of temperature

Compatibility: the measure of whether glass can be combined with other types of glass (or other materials) in the molten state and survive the cooling process without cracking

Crazing: a network of fine cracks in the surface of dichroic glass produced by the application of heat

Dichroic glass: iridescent glass that has a distinctly different color that changes with the light and angle at which it is viewed

Dots: small rounded bits of glass that are added to a bead randomly or in a pattern

Enamel paint: finely ground enamels mixed with water, oil, or acrylic-based medium

Enamel powder: a highly pigmented, finely crushed glass with more intense color than frit

Encasing: enclosing a bead or individual decorative elements with a layer of clear or transparent glass

Filigrana: rods with cores of opaque color encased with clear glass

Flame-anneal: slowly cooling glass to a certain temperature in the flame to partially relieve internal stress

Flame-cutting: using the torch to "cut" or separate sections of glass

Flashback: occurs when the flame burns back into the torch, hoses, and possibly the tanks

Frit: colored glass that has been crushed or ground into small bits in various grit sizes

Fuming: transferring gold or silver to a bead from a rod that has been charged with the metal, adding luster and sheen to the bead's surface

Fuse: to connect together by melting

Infinite control switch: a kiln switch that allows you to specify a general temperature range

Intense black glass: an opaque, true-black glass that spreads out on the surface of a bead to create a lacy, web-like effect when heated intensely

Internal mix or premix torch: a torch in which gases are mixed together within the body before emerging at the surface

Mandrel: a stainless-steel welding rod used to hold the wound molten glass that forms a bead

Marver: any non-flammable surface used to shape a hot bead

Mica powders (pixie dust): mica compounds in the form of superfine powders, which lend a pearly luster and metallic effect to beads

Millefiori: canes that are made by combining several glass rods or colors together, creating a cross-sectioned design when sliced

Oxidizing flame: a flame that is high in oxygen content

Pyrometer: a high-temperature thermometer that reads the kiln's internal temperature

Reducing flame: a flame that has a reduced amount of oxygen

Reduction: a type of flame chemistry in which the amount of oxygen is reduced in proportion to propane, producing what is known as a reduction flame with a reduction atmosphere

Reduction frit: made from glass that reacts chemically in a reduction atmosphere; coaxes a metallic response on a bead's surface

Set-point controller: a kiln device that keeps the temperature within a certain range

Soft glass: a term used to describe glass containing lead or soda-lime as flux, which has a much higher coefficient of expansion than hard glass

Strain temperature point: the lowest temperature at which glass can release stress

Striking colors: colored glass that is clear or transparent before being heated that changes color after being cooled to annealing temperature and then reheated to molten again

Stringer: a thin strand of glass that can be used to decorate beads in various ways

Surface mix torch: a torch that brings the gases to the surface where they are mixed as they emerge

Thermal shock: fracturing or breaking of glass caused by heating or cooling the glass too quickly

Trailing: the laying of threads or trails of hot glass over a glass object to form a decorative pattern

Twist: an advanced stringer form used to decorate beads

Artists' Index

Guest Artists

Kate Fowle Meleney has been lampworking beads since 1991 and teaching nationally and abroad since 1993. She has produced three instructional videos and is the subject of Jim Kervin's fourth in a series of booklets profiling contemporary glass beadmakers. Her collaboration with John Steinert helped to develop optic molds for beadmakers, and she worked with Thompson Enamels in 1996 to produce the 9000 series of enamels that are compatible with Effetre. She has been featured in such publications as *Lapidary Journal, Bead and Button, Glass Art,* and *Ornament.* (Photo by Jerry L. Anthony.)

Deanna Griffin Dove began her artistic career as a dancer and choreographer. She retired from the stage when she started a family. In 1995, her interests turned to glass beadmaking. Soon she was teaching beadmaking full-time all over the country. Her expertise and skill have led to her inclusion in several contemporary beadmaking books (including *1000 Glass Beads: Innovation & Imagination in Contemporary Glass Beadmaking,* Lark Books) as well as private and public museum collections. For more about her work and classes go to www.mindspring.com/~griffindove.

Index